LETTERS TO CARSON

LETTERS TO CARSON

JON OLBRYCH

A STORY WITHIN A STORY

gatekeeper press™
Columbus, Ohio

Letters to Carson: A Story Within a Story
Published by Gatekeeper Press
2167 Stringtown Rd, Suite 109
Columbus, OH 43123-2989
www.GatekeeperPress.com

The editorial work for this book is entirely the product of the author. Gatekeeper Press did not participate in and is not responsible for any aspect of this element.

Library of Congress Control Number: 2020949167

ISBN (paperback): 9781662906114
eISBN: 9781662906121

There is no greater feeling in the world than knowing you made a difference in someone's life. It could be for one minute, one day or for the rest of their life. You most likely will not know the impact of your actions in the moment or in your lifetime, so make it a point to be your best. Go with your gut, fight with conviction and be passionate about every moment you have been given. Find your purpose through trial and tribulation. Ask the tough questions and form your own opinions. Do not be heavily influenced. Keep your mind, body and spirit free so you can make an impact. Then, and only then will you be able to make the best choices and offer a helpful hand to those in need. Choose to live a good life and the path will become clear.

PREFACE

To my son, Carson,

YOU ARE THE INSPIRATION behind this book. I have always dreamed of publishing something. I am just an average guy, soon-to-be father, and in truth… I'm not even sure I would call this writing. It's more akin to documenting some of my life; just this collection of real world experiences that may leave you with more questions than you had when you started.

So why would you bother to read on? Because I'm your dad, and that means I'm awesome, and for better or for worse - I have a lot to say!

You'll find that a general theme in this self-proclaimed documentary of my short existence, is to be *interesting*. One of the only ways to become interesting is to actually go out and journey into the unknown; get out of your comfort zone.

To do that you'll need to be open-minded. Extend customs and courtesy to everyone you meet. Be thoughtful. When you're wrong, admit it… Well eventually at least! I am not a saint. I have had a hell of a life and it's only just really beginning now that you're on the way! I have made many mistakes, both small and large. I probably hurt some people without even knowing it or having a chance to say that I'm sorry.

But I don't dwell on those things. I make a conscious effort to learn and focus on improving myself, just a little

7

each time I see the opportunity. I want this for you as well. It's something that has helped me get through life: Accepting the good with the bad, and helping to build this world that you're being born into.

I also want you to know how truly wonderful it is to explore, to meet people from all walks of life, and to ask questions so that you can form your own opinions. This will help build your personal card catalogue (you'll have to look up what that is!) of experiences to share with *your* son one day!

In my life, I have many people who I am thankful for. Starting with my parents - your grandparents. I will never be able to fully explain to anyone just how lucky I am to be here today. Your grandparents are the reason why I strive for greatness on a daily basis.

By great I don't mean making loads of cash, driving a fancy car or becoming the President of the United States. Being great in everything you do really means that you're learning from your mistakes, that you're open to criticism.

Become friends with failure, because it's going to happen, and it too shall pass, and you're only using it as a means to evolve. Taking risks and making mistakes are tools you can use throughout life to become the version of yourself that you like most.

And then when you decide you want another updated version of yourself, you can do that too. Nothing is ever stagnant in this life.

You can be your own version of greatness if you put your mind, body, and soul into some of the most simple and mundane tasks. How you do anything becomes how you do everything. Just think: If you make it a point to work on one aspect of your life and improve upon it every day, you might be able to change your life or those who are in it.

I love my family and I am thankful to have an extremely intelligent sister who has put up with my shenanigans for thirty years! She went from the little sister who I pinned things on to a loving, kind-hearted, ambitious woman (a true friend) who I can go to for advice. I have many friends, colleagues, and mentors whom I have had the privilege of learning from along the way. These people inspired me, motivated me, or influenced me in profound, permanent ways - and they continue to guide me, even through this process of becoming your father.

For now, here's a few guidelines to reading this journal. First, I have a feeling that I'll probably read this to you many times before you understand a single word. Your beautiful mother Susana has yet to read any of this. In fact, she is unaware I'm even writing this journal. I have been writing it during her pregnancy - while she is busy growing *you*. I've been working on it in the early morning and late-night hours when I can't seem to sleep; these are often moments when I have a lot on my mind.

Second, there is something very special included in the middle of this journal which I will most likely skip over until you are old enough to understand. That is the journal that I kept while I served overseas fighting in Fallujah, Iraq. I am proud to say that your mom and I both were members of the greatest fighting force on this Earth, the United States Marine Corps. I kept a journal while on a seven-month tour in Iraq. Some of the language is raw, crude, and downright inappropriate for even some adults. For that reason, I plan on skipping that part until you are older.

With that being said, I finally read *that* journal from cover to cover and was able to transcribe it to a computer so it won't ever be lost. It paints a very realistic picture of what my actual thoughts were while serving in our military. To be honest, I haven't shared that previous journal with anyone to this day. After reading it and having to pause at several points, I knew this was how I wanted to share it with you and anyone else who wanted to read it. I was so scared at times. I was so sad at others.

That sadness sticks with me to this day because I served with some great men. Some of them made the ultimate sacrifice while fighting for our country and our way of life. Just remember to always be respectful of our military members, and learn about what Veterans Day and Memorial Day symbolize. I hope you will be a proud American, like your dad. We live in the most prosperous and privileged country in the world where many people have become blind to it.

Finally, have fun. Live your life to the fullest because you only get one. Sorry, but it's true. If you have a crappy day and everything is crashing all around you, go to sleep, so you can wake up tomorrow, because tomorrow is another day. Then... believe it or not, there's a day after that too!

You won't be able to change the past, but you can always do things that may impact the future, or even just the present moment. Don't forget to enjoy at least some little thing every day. When the going gets tough, think: Somebody out there has it much worse than you, and it's only as tough as you let your mind make it. Instead of sitting in the corner pouting, stand up tall and take a deep breath. Then, come up with a plan to change the course. It's not worth it to sit around feeling sorry for yourself! If you can master this skill and the mindset that comes with it, you just might inspire others to follow your lead.

Great leaders lead from the front. You, Carson, can be a great leader if you give it all you got!

Love, Dad

23 SEPTEMBER 2018

Dear Carson,

I have re-typed this first sentence almost 5 times now so I guess I'll just say, hey buddy! It's Sunday night and I have had quite the weekend. Something really special happened. I found out who you were!

I have spent a lot of my free time just sitting in the car or at work daydreaming about who you were going to be. What are you going to be like? Who will look like? How are you going to sound? However, that is pretty tough to do 100% when there is one really important thing missing.

Your mom and I decided a week ago that we could not wait another 6 weeks to find out if you were a boy or a girl! So, we woke up extra early on Saturday so we could go to this really cool place that does ultrasounds. Another special part of the trip was that I booked a very special hotel room located at Port Orleans in the French Quarter at Disney! It was the start of her "birthday week." We were packed and ready to go for an adventure of a weekend that included relaxing, the Food and Wine Festival at Epcot and of course, the ultrasound!!!

We were delayed after I was stung behind the ear by a hornet, but with a precise appointment block, I knew we couldn't be late! I drove your mom to the place, which was in a very nice little plaza overlooking a small man-made lake with a water fountain. The lobby had a nice little reception counter and the room was painted in tranquil colors with baby photos hung nicely in different areas. We got the go ahead to enter through the hallway to the ultrasound room. Subtle calming music was playing and a comfy lounge chair was there waiting for us. After a quick introduction with the technician, we got right to it! "It's a boy."

I'll tell you what, it was one of the most exciting moments of my life, the second the ultrasound lady said those words. If having our first child wasn't exciting enough, finding out your gender made it even more amazing. I can't wait to meet you, hold you, love you and teach you as much as possible!

I decided about two weeks ago, while I was sitting at the very desk I'm at now, that I need to do something different. I have been wanting to publish something for years. It has been one of the goals I've always had. I have written and journaled on and off over the years during my time in the military and some in between. However, life happened in that time. There were some ups and downs and all arounds. I have seen some pretty awe-inspiring things. I've had the opportunity to meet some amazing people and learn from mentors along the way. I have had to observe horrific things no person should ever have to. I have had to overcome battles both physically and emotionally. I have witnessed people go on to accomplish great things with their lives. I've seen great people and some not so great people have their lives unfortunately cut short.

I have had this urge, this push, this drive to write you a letter a day until you are born so that I can maybe share some of the stories and events of my life. I also want to share with you some of my feelings and emotions that go through my mind for the next 150 or so days till we get to meet face to face for the first time. I hope that's ok and that one day you'll maybe do something similar for your son or daughter. If anything, my intention is not to school you, not to preach to you but just to share. I want you to learn about who your father is, how I think and what emotions I've had to endure through a roller-coaster ride of this thing called life.

Life is a beautiful thing. This is the first of probably many cliché comments and sayings that will pop up throughout my letters to you. Guess what! That's not a bad thing! So, prepare yourself! Prepare yourself for little quotes, dorky comments and funny moments. I hope you find a way to laugh at some of the things I share with you, as well as maybe cry. Learn some things and learn some things to not do. Maybe this will be a tool for you to go back and look at every once in a while, just to think, hmm, what would my dad do? *Disclaimer: that might not always be the best choice--nor the second or third choice!*

A sad, *very small* reason I wanted to start writing this was because every day there is a chance it might be your last...Yes, I am aware it's another cliché. Get over it! If I am not around when you are born or hey, even if you are born and it's in the early years, you might not have the ability to make memories of me. This book, novel, or whatever it will be is the chance for me to write to you so that you can know your father. That's a pretty neat thing and so is the life you're given.

Till tomorrow, Carson.   ....

24 SEPTEMBER 2018

Hey Buddy! ....

First thing, just writing that first line, as cheesy as it may sound, made my day so much better. I have been looking forward to writing to you in the back of my mind all day. I thought about what I was going to write on the way into work. I have a very long commute. One hour and twenty minutes, actually. It's a peaceful and easy ride, but it is very long! I tend to do most of my thinking to and from work. In the morning, I think about all types of things. My mind wanders and it used to be that I wrote notes so that I could remember what thoughts I had so I could put them to paper later on. Days can be very busy and filled with all types of noise and distractions. Noise being positive, negative and anything in between. Among all of *that* you find yourself constantly learning, listening, improving, making mistakes and so on.

Recently, I have noticed that I've been pausing to think after I complete a task or have disagreements with people I interact with. Maybe it's crazy, but I find that I have been thinking about you! How can I be a better person, a better listener? How would I teach my son, *you*, in the moment? I once wrote in one of my many unpublished works that never saw the finish line that "my mind is my weapon now and my pen is my first line of defense." The first part of that is very true. Physical gifts and talents can only get you so far. I used to fight with my fists, my rifle, tactics and maneuvers, trained by the best of the best. But I will always remember that it's those few extra seconds you let your mind and your instincts take over that will decide the best outcome in many situations. There will be plenty of letters where I will tell you more about that, I promise!

Carson, you will be a strong, fair and honest young man if you are able to think for yourself and be true to your heart. Today was one of my longer and more unpleasant days I've had in a long time. I am a teacher and trainer, but not the kind you'll know of for quite some time. I train both military and Federal Police in weapons and tactics for a living. At times, like today, I had lots of people come through my classes and I barely had a chance to relax, pause or even eat lunch!

I found out later in the day that a very close friend of mine's mother passed away. It really hurt me knowing I could not be around for him since he lives very far away. Feeling like you can't help will be something you feel time and time again in your life. You'll want to be there for close friends, family and even strangers at times. Especially when they are in pain, both physically and emotionally. Sometimes being there to support someone in their darkest and most unpleasant moments can impact their lives so much so that it helps them from making bad decisions. At the very least, being a good friend is one of the most important traits anyone can have. Listen to people and let them tell you about what hurts them. It might make a bigger difference than you'll ever know.

I went to the gym after my long drive home today. Your dad is very badass and thinks he's still in the Marine Corps and can hang with the 23-year-old version of himself! I can picture your beautiful mom laughing reading this right now. The funny part is that she would be shaking you because you are just a tiny little fella inside her right now! I promise I will be writing more about her, your grandma and grandpa in the days to come.

At the gym I was finishing up my workout on the tread-mill. I looked over the balcony where the cardio machines are set up so they overlook the whole gym and saw something really special. I saw a woman who was in a wheelchair being helped by her husband. She was using a rowing type machine and her husband moved her legs ever so gently so she could be helped back into her wheelchair after her final set. I couldn't help but think to myself how special and how in love they must be. What a good man he was to stick by her side and how strong his wife must be to feel no shame to enjoy the little things in life together. Working with each other, they didn't even seem to skip a beat. I thought of your mom and I. Sometimes we have our moments, like most couples do. However, I know I'd be right there for her every single day I'm alive to help her if we were ever in that situation. We are a great team and I know we will sacrifice together so that you will have the best life possible! Goodnight Carson, see you soon!

25 SEPTEMBER 2018

Hey Bubba,

I'm just thinking about a few things today. I was on my way home today after a stressful day at work and found myself becoming upset, even angry, with my dad. The weird part about it is that I was discussing him and my mom coming to visit you once you are born! I was upset because your grandparents were wanting to come down and see you after you were born instead of for Christmas and your baby shower like we had already planned. When I write it out, it sounds so dumb.

I let my emotions get the best of me and I yelled and cursed at my dad. He didn't deserve it because he was trying to explain why the plans he was mentioning made more sense. My frustrations had nothing to do with the timeline at all.

After we hung up the phone, I immediately felt terrible. That was my dad, the man who has gone out of his way, along with my mom, to ensure I have had the life I am living now. I know my emotions are mostly because I miss them. I miss my family because I live in Florida and they are 1500 miles away in Connecticut. The last time I saw them was January 20th for my and Susana's wedding.

I realized a few things in this moment, once the call ended and I turned the radio in my car back up louder than anyone should have it. One, my parents aren't going to be around forever. Sure, I have known this, but when you realize that every time you see them might be the last, it kind of weighs on you. I average being able to see my mom, dad and sister Kristen about twice a year. That is one of the only regrets that I have, living down in Florida and choosing to leave Ridgefield, Connecticut, where they all still reside or in close proximity.

Next, I realized that time is valuable regardless of how you spend it. Make sure to try and make amends as soon as you can. Make it a point to not hold grudges and swallow your pride. Say I'M SORRY! for God's sake. I want you to learn about your grandfather and grandmother so I will write about them shortly. I am a very lucky person and if it weren't for them, I wouldn't be here. It's not in the way you would think, either. Ultimately, a lot of the reasons I have made the choices I have are because of the life they gave me. I will always be grateful and make it a point to make them proud of me every day!

Love you buddy! Can't wait to meet you!

26 SEPTEMBER 2018

Hey little guy,

So, your mom told me that you were the size of a donut today and it made me laugh. She has a really good habit of saying really funny things at sometimes inappropriate times. It's one of my favorite little things that we share as a couple. Our sense of humor is a little different, but I think it works. I tell her to stop laughing when we are hanging out relaxing because I know she's shaking you! I'll yell "STOP, you're going to make scrambled eggs in there!" It's a disturbing image I suppose, but it works. If one of our three dogs accidentally puts a paw up or sticks their nose in her stomach your mom or I will yell, "DON'T POKE THE BABY!"

Anyway, today's lesson is about confidence and the ability to project yourself in a positive way! I just finished up an interview for a police training job for NASA. I now know that I don't want to be a police trainer for NASA! The interview started off pretty well, other than the fact that I was blind-sided by three individuals rather than the one I was expecting.

They asked a few basic questions to start; about my background, why did I want the job…Then it hit me, I didn't really know what the job was! From the job description that I had reviewed a few times and the internet searches, I was able to determine that it was some kind of trainer position. Great, come to find out that this job was for a lead instructor at NASA's own police academy (similar to the one that I went through to get my police certification years ago).

Well, it's safe to say your dad was not prepared! On top of that they explained in the following questions that there would be a travel requirement for around 16 weeks per year and up to two weeks at a time. This far exceeded my interpretation of the job description that said *some travel may be required.* At that moment I knew this job wasn't for me. I knew I was working on my Master's Degree and wanted to get away from law enforcement and certainly didn't want to teach police recruits while being away from you and your mom!

This is where the confidence came into play. I was nervous; I think everyone gets nervous when they are put on the spot, at least a little. Even though this was a job I knew 10 minutes into the interview I did not want, I still wanted to impress these gentlemen. I wanted to answer their sometimes broad and mostly direct questions to the best of my ability.

When I say best of my ability I mean that if you have no stinking clue, make it sound like you have some idea. Certainly, don't sit there and do the whole "UM, UM, UM" thing and stare blankly while sweat starts to build. Repeat the question back and think of something kind of relevant to say! These guys were good. They asked specific weapons questions. They asked me about making lesson plans for things I never taught. They asked me 3 specific case law questions, only one of which sounded even remotely familiar. I tried, though! When I was completely stumped, I would pause, collect myself and say, "I will go find out the answer to that, I need to brush up on that case or subject."

The takeaway here is that I am really good at my current job, a weapons and tactics instructor for the Department of the Air Force. I enjoy teaching people and passing on information just as much as I enjoy learning from others. I learned from this interview that I could review some of those subjects I was asked about. More importantly, I gained valuable experience for my next interview. My goal is to eventually get into another career field. The strategy is to progress in my career so that I can help support our family as much as possible. I'd like to advance my knowledge in fields that I am not so familiar with. It's important to learn a little about as many subjects as possible.

Another of the big life skills is the ability to think quickly and project your thoughts clearly. That's a trait that if mastered, can take you to new limits! Although I walked away from the interview with immediate uncertainty of my performance, it was not until writing to you that I realized something. Confidence and the ability to put your best foot forward, even if it's something you don't necessarily want, can still serve as a valuable tool on the road to victory.

I love you, Carson!

27 SEPTEMBER 2018

Hey big guy! ....

Today was a long day. I stayed busy at work, but it was a little sad because it was the last day for one of the Airmen that I work with. He is heading on to another assignment, so it is exciting for him. This year marks the 4th year that I have worked in the Combat Arms section at Patrick Air Force Base and the 45th Security Forces Squadron as a Civilian Instructor. I have had the opportunity to work with lots of inspiring and motivated individuals both military and civilian. In terms of the Airmen that I've worked with, everyone that was there for my first day has now officially moved on to different assignments, bases and places around the world. That's the military for you. You don't know when your number is going to be called and you have to always be prepared for the unexpected.

Today, I walked out to begin my weekend, which I already knew would have a lot to do with getting things ready for you! I realized that you will have people come into your life that will be there to help you be successful, or even just be people you see on a regular basis. Hopefully as you grow, you will have so many opportunities to build relationships that you will always remember. It used to be that when people left, you really couldn't keep in touch with them unless you had their new address and maybe visited every so often. Now, with the help of the major social media platforms, people may leave for a place halfway around the world, but you'll still know what they are having for dinner or when they are going to the gym. Yes, I am talking about people that upload pictures of the food they eat or stand in front of the mirror at the gym. I have a feeling that once you're old enough, social media will still be a thing. Maybe with more virtual interaction. *Scary!*

I guess what I realized is that when people come and go in your life, especially the ones you care about, you wish them the very best. I think it is essential to make every effort to keep them in your life even if it's an email every so often, a phone call once a month or just following them on social media. If you have to leave a familiar place and everything you know, especially for the first time, that will be very helpful in your transition to the next chapter of your life.

Keep your friends close as you build new relationships. My best man Kenny, for example; he lives in Maine! I still try to talk to him on the phone every so often. Even though we both have relocated multiple times over our 25-year friendship, through the Marine Corps for me and his nationwide coaching assignments, we manage to always meet back up somehow, someway.

As for co-workers, learn from them, embrace their different approaches to tasks and assignments. They may show you new and innovative ways to accomplish goals and objectives. Likewise, you may be able to show them methods or your own way of thinking that they had overlooked. If you move on in your career, be sure to thank the people that helped you get there. Maybe at some point you will be in a position to offer them a job, or be a reference in a position that they apply for. Professional networking might be the key to landing that dream job one day. I was a little late to that game and never realized how valuable it is until recent years.

I'll leave you with this. Every day is the chance to change your life or someone else's. Through interaction with others, you can bring out the best in other people and their best will push you to levels you didn't think existed. Embrace friends and coworkers. Your attitude and disposition can and will influence the outcome of your day!

Carson, you will do great things!   ....

28 SEPTEMBER 2018

Hey little man,

Today I am going to write about the perfect woman.

The perfect woman is honest and truthful. She has no issue telling you when you are wrong. To some guys, this might be the *last* thing they want in a woman. I am not making a definitive statement about what traits and characteristics are the most important. I am however, making sure to include this one because it was the first of many that come to mind. A truthful woman will have no problem letting you or others know you are in the wrong *or* in the right, for that matter. They will be your biggest supporter. They will fight to get you back on track and in many cases stand right by your side as you become stronger together because of it.

The perfect woman has the ability to compromise. It's one of the most difficult things to do! If a woman can compromise and make sacrifices on her side she is *beyond* a keeper! Whenever a woman shows a tendency to compromise, I have felt even more of a reason to find the middle ground on my end. In fact, I might rethink the argument or even submit completely. That this statement can be very quickly refuted, since I happen to be a stubborn Aries! In most cases, I do not go down without a fight and I know from many years of experience that I am as tenacious as they come.

It's not always about winning an argument or disagreement. It is, however, about knowing that the woman you are with can always bring strong and helpful opposing views to the table. It's at that point that you will know she's the one. On many occasions, I have sat back in admiration of a woman and watched her go toe to toe over things she believes in. She has the ability to silence the entire room with educated, robust knowledge, backed by facts to make her point clear. That's one hell of a woman!

The perfect woman has the ability to shine in a way that is hard to describe. When in a public setting she smiles. By her smiling, others are mesmerized not just by her physical beauty, but by how genuine she is. Glowing isn't the word I would always use here, but I'll tell you, that woman can light up the deepest darkest cave twenty thousand feet under the ocean. Hopefully the point has been made, son!

The perfect woman supports your goals as she works diligently to pursue her own. Sometimes those goals are shared by both people. Other times, you might have these "brilliant" ideas and she will smile, nod her head and listen to your ambitious rant. She will know right away that your drive and resilience in achieving success in all that you do will ultimately pay off. A strong woman by your side should motivate you and won't always be dependent on you. When it comes to goals, you won't need to worry about her and she won't need your validation in pursuit of the next big thing!

The perfect woman has a heart of gold. She is willing to comfort you in your darkest moments. She's your support and is as upset as you are when you are hurting. She wants things to work out for you more than you do at times. She'll put her own pain and discomfort on the sidelines as she checks into the game to save the team! She is a hero. She is strong and her compassion for others is the biggest characteristic you'll want to emulate. Sometimes you'll watch as she works her subtle magic and puts herself before others. Hell, she'll come to your assistance even when you hurt yourself in the most ridiculous of ways, including falling through a seat at a movie theater and breaking two toes!

The perfect woman catches your eye from across the room. She's not necessarily wearing the ball gown with a plunging neckline and showing off her tan, long, model-esque legs. She can make you stop what you're doing, including the deep conversation that you are in. She'll make you notice her simply sitting off to the side drinking coffee and reading a book. Under the dim reading light, she'll make you look even harder as you admire the simple beauty and the subtle peace she's at with every page she turns. Similarly, this woman can be in a group setting and, as mentioned before, has a constant smile on her face. She has eyes that are soft yet stunning and they draw you in. You want to find out more about her. You almost want to have what she has in the sense of pure fluidity and poise in every moment. You'll realize you keep being drawn back to her because her presence makes you weak. You can't quite finish your thoughts. The coordination that you might have had at the beginning of the night somehow got away from you without you even realizing. She'll approach you and all you can do is stumble over the few coherent words that manage to escape your lips. She has you. She is a beauty.

That perfect woman might not be perfect, but she's perfect for me. That perfect woman is your mom.

29 SEPTEMBER 2018

Big Guy!

Today is going to be a great day. Your mom and I are going to start working on your room! We knew moving into our house that we would need 4 bedrooms because we wanted to start a family one day. Well, that day is right around the corner! Your room has been used for all types of awesome things. It was once the storage room when your mom and I were way too exhausted to sort out moving boxes when we first moved into the house. We finally cleared out about 75 percent of the crap and then someone had the bright idea to make your room the wedding room. Some crazy people I know decided that moving during one of the worst hurricanes (Irma) while trying to plan a wedding would be an awesome idea!

For the record, and your mom will always attest to this, your dad has always been a bit of a bull in a china shop. I tend to be one of the most scatter-brained people around. I can go a thousand miles in one direction just to turn ninety degrees and start running as fast as I can, chasing a new idea. I think that you'll probably be able to pick up on that as you read along!

For that first year, your room was also my workout room. It had my BoFlex Ultimate workout machine that I purchased from a garage sale for a decent price. It's fair to say it was used about once a month. And yes, as you read this, please imagine your mom laughing because it's true. I still think that I'm the 23-year-old Marine who can run 3 miles in 18 minutes and do 20 pull-ups after a night partying with the boys without being phased. In your dad's first ever confession, I might have lost a step or two! I may not be in the Marine shape I once was but I can still hold my own. So, just remember that. Like my father, who is the size of an NFL linebacker at 6 foot 5 and 240 pounds, there will always be a part of me that knows he can take me down. So *please*, have a teenage outburst or god forbid, use profanity in the direction of your mother who is a saint. If she doesn't come at you like a spider monkey you better believe the raging bull is right behind her! You hit the jackpot buddy, both your parents are Marines! Believe it or not we both still believe in the Core Values and the many other principles Marines are taught from their early days at basic training.

So, in conclusion, we can't wait to start working on your dinosaur nursery today. It will be so much fun going to Home Depot to pick out colors for the walls!

I Love you Carson, you'll be just fine.

30 SEPTEMBER 2018

What's up, buddy?

I'm here at my desk at zero dark thirty and figured I'd write your letter early rather than late in the day as I usually do. I was listening to the radio on the way in to work and it's scary where the media is taking this country. It is so divided. I won't get *too* political since you'll have all the time in the world to try and make sense of that whole abomination.

It's sad that people vote or think only along party lines. If you're a conservative thinker you must *love* guns and the second amendment. If you're a liberal, well, you must want the government to give you *everything* and take care of you while you cry because you can't find a job. More importantly, I think it's really important to do your own research. Listen to people with opposing views. Watch documentaries that are far right wing and those that are far left wing. Look up specific issues and see what people are doing about it. Who is involved? Who is making an actual effort to fix something? Some people might only be doing it for a political statement or to collect illegal campaign money. I'm not saying get involved with politics and fight with opposing sides. I do however, feel that you should always be able to voice your opinion no matter the setting as long as you are respectful. Support your conversation with facts. Don't follow the media since they will always show their own version of a story. Instead, put on both CNN and Fox next to each other and realize that they are both helping divide the country. One will be slamming a president while the other will be saying he's the best thing in the world.

I think our country is becoming more and more divided because of the culture we have created, Americans are no longer happy with a simple and basic way of life. The idea of the American dream is alive and well, yet people on both sides of the aisle want to create this notion that one is going to corrupt the other. If there isn't any change it will be bad, if there is too much change, we'll be ruined. Meanwhile, remember that America is easily the wealthiest country in the world. The United States has the greatest military. America, in its short existence, has granted more freedom and spread the idea of Democracy while bringing the most people out of poverty than any nation in the world. America leads the world in innovation, technology, medicine, sports and entertainment. Countries around the world try to follow our example and many of the countries that denounce American prosperity and the westernized way of life often keep their people left far behind.

America is great because you have the right and the ability to make your own decisions. You have the right to vote on issues. Vote with your heart but ALWAYS vote. In America, you have the greatest right of them all, freedom of speech. Embrace it, but don't abuse it. In some cases, I have seen people try their very hardest to stop people from speaking only to push one agenda. It is very prevalent right now on college campuses like UC Berkeley. Whenever there is a conservative speaker going to talk to campus Republican groups they have in most cases been met with violence and protests. Freedom of speech also means that you have the freedom to NOT listen. I have seen a very strong movement over the last 8 years to try and silence any conservative conferences when they come up. It seems the anti-Republican movement will stop at nothing, including violence, to not allow free speech. Again, this is just what I have witnessed and how I have interpreted what is shown on TV and in social media.

Have pride in being an American. Many men and women gave their lives protecting our way of life both in nations far away and here at home, taking an oath to serve and protect. Remember, in America there are stories of people making it from the very bottom, spending their last dollar and taking the biggest leap of faith to achieve greatness. These Americans are proud to live in a country with more rags to riches stories than any other country on the planet. It's very safe to say they wouldn't have that chance in many other places.

American citizens, old and young, take for granted all the luxuries we have. We live in a world where we have internet access 24 hours a day, smartphones and cars. We don't know what it's like to live without air conditioning or clean water, yet people, including celebrities and very wealthy people threaten to leave as social media warriors. They act mad and upset at the very country that provided the opportunity to achieve whatever success they set out for themselves. We don't live in a communist society and luckily, we never had to witness starvation and plague. People all around the world dream of coming to America and seeing that beautiful Statue of Liberty and the numerous National Landmarks from sea to shining sea! We forget the very basic principles that are instilled in us at the early days of our lives.

Be a good person. Listen to *everyone,* including opposing viewpoints. Learn a little about everything. Be interesting! Take pride in your accomplishments and always set new goals. Don't take that opportunity for granted. You will be so successful if you work hard, treat people with respect and if

JON OLBRYCH

they don't like what you have to say that's ok. Be the bigger
person and don't let it get to the point where you are physical unless you are protecting yourself, your family or friends
from physical harm. Then, and only then, kick some ass.
Your family comes first. Always.

One day closer.

1 OCTOBER 2018

Hey Tater Tot,

That's what your mom and I once called you when you were the size of the awesome snack food. We have these apps on our phones that track the pregnancy process week to week, day by day. Yes, I know what you will be thinking one day; Dad, that's stupid, we're guys, why would you have apps like that. Well, to start, I had no clue they existed before your mom, who is a goddess of the internet, phone and all things Pinterest. I was told, for the sake of trying to keep this letter PG, to download these apps AND LEARN SOMETHING! So here I am, getting daily updates of the changes that are going through your mom's body, what your approximate height and weight are and even a comparison to you and some obscure object. I'll elaborate.

The Bump app is very pink in its design and layout, making any man who has it have that little sense to make sure no other guys are around when he goes to look at it! This is by no means an embarrassing thing, considering I have other apps downloaded to my phone that all do pretty much the same damn thing.

So, the Bump app says today (week 15) that "baby is as big as a navel orange." Yeah, I don't make this stuff up and trust me, it gets even stranger in the descriptions. Week twelve you were the size of a plum and were 2.09 inches weighing an amazing .49 ounces. You were a blueberry in week seven. Week two, the first week the app gave us an idea you were as big as a banana seed. The app ends at the end, the most exciting point, when we get to meet you! The last comparison, thank God, week 40, says you are as big as a watermelon!

Let's have a little more fun with this, since who knows if apps will even be a thing when you're old enough to understand all this. It's crazy to think about it, but believe it or not I was once a kid and although computers were in the very early stages, I didn't have a computer in my house till I was in middle school. I hand-wrote everything school-related and wrote in cursive. We had landlines in the house with long cords so that we could walk approximately 15 feet from the phone. At one point, I had a phone that looked like a basketball! Your grandpa once got a company car that had a car phone in it and I remember calling my mom on it, thinking it was the craziest thing in the world. To be honest, it was. I am pretty sure that two- to three-minute conversation from the car phone probably cost $20-$30!

I used to have to type my papers on a typewriter and your grandma would proofread my horrible spelling, terrible grammar and made-up words with a nice red pen and tell me to do it again. I usually needed at least three drafts before I could even think about being done. Although I don't miss the typewriter or writing in *the lost art* of cursive, I know that all those corrections and frustrating drafts made me better overall. I learned to think a little more before putting words to paper and to edit my own work. I also learned that not everything can be rushed and just turned in without a second or third look. I learned to take pride in my work because of all the time and effort I put into it. I'll never forget my dad always giving me a folder and saying to turn in my papers with a nice clear cover or at least in a nice folder. This was great advice that I still use to this day. If you work hard to put something together you should shine it up and present it the best way possible. It shows the character of the author.

I suppose that one day you'll laugh when I mention that I played outside and went on adventures in my backyard growing up. I wasn't allowed to have video games growing up, although I asked for some every year for Christmas. I made forts with branches and made bows and arrows out of random crap. I played day-long games of manhunt with all the neighbors. My buddies and I would set out on adventures on our bikes. We would find or make trails through the nearby woods. We even had a mountain bike course that had steep hills and jumps that we would try our best not to get seriously injured showing off on.

One day, when a flash flood occurred, I was with my good friend Even. Instead of going inside, I had the brilliant idea of throwing my hat in one of the storm runoff drains. To make matters worse, we figured it was a great idea to jump into the surging water after it. What started off as us floating down 3ft or so of water in a rapid that easily carried us downstream turned into narrow channels under cement cauldrons with water rising over our heads in some places. We went under fences, grabbed on to branches to pause and take in the adventure we were on. The rain, accompanied with thunder and lighting, continued and so did we. Our adventure came to an end when we reach an impassable flowing river that was at least 50 feet across. At that point we realized that maybe we should turn it around. It was getting a bit dangerous! Not realizing that the river that we had intersected was overflowing and going over many of the surrounding roads, we followed the side of storm runoff back in the direction we came. Once we found a fence, we followed the fence line to the closest road to hopefully catch our bearings and get some idea of where we were. Then, in the distance we saw a road, a cul-de-sac actually. We headed that way and just as we got there, we were met by our parents honking the car horn angrily. Well, I don't need to tell you how this one turned out. You can use your judgement. I might have been grounded for a few days and reminded that I was never allowed out in the middle of a violent rainstorm again. Days later, once released from house arrest, I made my way over to Even's where the storm drain had diminished down to just a slow moving, one-foot deep stream and there it was. My hat, wedged under a rock and a couple branches.

Have fun Carson, get dirty, go explore, but please be safe and use your judgement! Sometimes that gut instinct will keep you safe or alive. Guess what, video games still weren't as cool as some of the real-life adventures I've been a part of. In fact, they now make video games based on some of the things I've done and seen. I'll save that for another day.

Till next time!

3 OCTOBER 2018

Hey Carson,

Today I was driving to work as I normally do. The road to work is very peaceful with water on both sides for the most part. Although my commute is longer than I or any normal human being would enjoy, I tend to make the best of it. Oftentimes I find myself listening to audiobooks on topics like finance, investing or interesting people like Elon Musk and Steve Jobs. I have always been very fascinated with the large companies like Google, Apple, Facebook and Amazon. They seem to be taking over the world in both good and bad ways.

I love technology and innovation. I love success stories and behind every one of these huge companies is a struggle. Where did they all begin and what kind of madman knew that one day this whole Internet thing would run our lives? Seriously, I was a little boy when I first watched the movie Terminator starring Arnold Schwarzenegger. In that classic movie robots eventually take over the world. In some cases, I feel that is the direction we are going!

The Internet wasn't even a thing when I was young and now it is most likely the most relied upon thing we have today. I can do everything online and on a computer. Better yet, I can *Google* the answer to anything from my phone wherever in the world I am! I am able to purchase almost anything I want while I'm at work and have it waiting for me at home thanks to Amazon. And then there's Facebook. With Mark Zuckerberg's often-criticized creation, I can see what one of my old military buddies and his family are doing to enjoy a family vacation to Disney World with one scroll of the news feed. Everyone has either an Android or an Apple iPhone, period. Apple is the luxury, cool and hip phone, Apple itself was successful in branding its products as innovative, sophisticated and classy. They own the phone and laptop market by a long shot and even have brick and mortar stores that *are super cool and trendy* if you're into Apple products.

So basically, these big companies that pretty much run the world in the consumer space are a product of people with a vision. The CEOs of these companies, other than having *bajillions* of dollars, have the ability to take their companies in whatever direction they want. They can possibly change history and the status quo. I am taking classes online right now at the Florida Institute of Technology. I think that there has been a shift where something like 35% of all degrees are accomplished online. I don't think it's too crazy to think that Google and Apple could team up one day and create something like a Google University or an Apple Institute.

I see the decline in infrastructure in our country in certain areas, especially retail. Large shopping malls are a thing of the past since everyone shops online for 90% of the things they need. Hell, people now have their groceries delivered to them after some person goes down the aisles and does the shopping for them. So, in essence, I see a lot of these malls becoming completely vacant and obsolete. This is where the innovation continues and making the best of a bad thing begins. I can see these malls across the country turn into learning centers ran by these large companies like Google and Apple. The costs would be low and they would ultimately force universities to lower their costs of astronomically high tuition. *That is another real problem in the country!* These malls turned into education meccas would teach innovative areas in computing, Information Technology, Special technical fields like radiology and computer-based programs. That is where the future is and where the jobs are going to be.

Robotics has come a long way and as we see in Amazon mega-distribution centers that robots can run at 3 to 5 times the speed of a person and run for 24 hours nonstop. They can be programmed to do multiple tasks at one time and basically cut out the need for humans. This is not a bad thing. It just means you might want to look into the field of robot repair and maintenance!

I think that if you are savvy and aware of your surroundings, if you read and always try to learn a little more about different subjects, you'll be able to take on the world. No matter the direction you go and whatever new technology becomes available, you will never be able to lose sight of your own intellect. Your instincts and abilities to think on your own, learn from mistakes will allow you to imagine places you want to go and accomplish anything you want to do. Carson, you will be a rockstar!

5 OCTOBER 2018

Carson,

Howdy! Today I want to talk about my wedding day and a few other things that just make me happy. It was the first thing that came to mind. Man was it awesome. As any husband is supposed to say, it was the best day of my life. Unfortunately, I have always used that phrase for all sorts of crap. But unsurprisingly this last year might have actually been the best year of my life!

Let's see...all the "best days of my life" that I can remember from this last year. Yes, I am going on a tangent as I usually do. It's part of my problem! I asked your mom to marry me at the top of the Tower of the Americas in San Antonio, TX. *Best day ever.* She said yes, by the way! I will let her reenact the moment since it involves your very nervous dad looking quite sick! Even trying to rehearse a few times in the bathroom I might have still frozen up and mumbled about ten words that were not really English! She sure did look pretty though!

Your mom and I planned a wedding (she'll say she did most of it) through selling my house and being homeless living in our good friend Jared and Christy's guest room through a mega hurricane (Irma). But, that feeling we had when we were standing in front of our home, the one that you'll be welcomed into with open arms, was the *best day ever*. Standing at the altar that I built watching your mom walk down the aisle in the rustic, relaxing Danville Bed and Breakfast officially was the *best day ever*.

I'll tell you what, about 20 minutes before, I needed to wipe away tears because I got to do a no look picture with your mom. The photographer, Margie, positioned your mom on one side of a door in the beautiful building where she and her bridesmaids were getting ready. I walked in, practically on a leash to ensure I did not see the bride! The moment I knew that my soon to be wife, who I had not seen or heard from all day, was only separated by an inch of mahogany I felt weak. When I put my hand out and she took my hand with a few people watching us smiling as the photos were taken, I officially could not hold back. I got choked up knowing how much I loved your mom and how that truly was the *best day ever*.

I was standing in my underwear on the balcony of our private, super suite bungalow in Cancun on our "mini-moon" right after the Eagles won the NFC Championship game. I looked at the ocean as it was only 20 feet away from me and looked back into our tropical romance pad and your mom was sitting on the bed laughing at me and it was the *best day ever*.

After pulling up to the police headquarters at Cape Canaveral AFS, I was about to get out of the police truck that I was using to pick up weapons for my work. With my boss, sitting next to me I received a text message saying "can you talk?" This was unusual and I quietly stepped out of the truck and gave her a call. Your mom answered and again she asked, "are you able to talk and are you alone?" "YES, what is it? Is everything okay," I said kind of quietly. "We're pregnant." And it was *the best day ever*.

Talk to you soon bubba. I love you!

9 OCTOBER 2018

I love you guys so much. You can accomplish anything in life if you're willing to work for it. Let that sink in for a minute. That was what Drew Brees said last night as his kids joined him on the football field as he became the all-time passing leader in NFL history.

Your mom and I are huge football fans. We watch football every Sunday and in time, you'll have to decide if you are going to be a Philadelphia Eagles fan or a New Orleans Saints fan! I have been a lifelong Eagles fan dating back to my very first live sporting event at Veteran's Stadium in Philadelphia. When I was adopted, your grandparents were living in Lancaster County, PA about 30 minutes or so outside of Philly. There are some early memories of my birthday parties with a few friends at Eagles games. There I took photos with the Eagles cheerleaders and the Eagles mascot Swoop.

Knowing not a whole lot about the game and just cheering when others did, I eventually found myself living in Texas after my dad took a job that relocated our family. Things changed in Texas when I got booed for wearing my Eagles shirt at school. I was starting to understand what rivalries were. I was in Cowboys Country. Philadelphia and the Dallas Cowboys had a long-standing division rivalry and the Cowboys were right in their prime in the early 90's. They had won their infamous 3 Super Bowls all very close together in '93,'94 and '96. This is why my generation has so many damn Cowboys fans. Most of them (the cowgirls' fans) have never been to Texas, let alone a live Cowboys game *in Dallas*. Either way, my blood still ran Eagles green, for whatever small connection I had with the team I feel is more American-sounding than Dallas ever will be. It's said that Dallas is "America's Team." Again, like most, it can be argued that the Eagles are from the city where the Constitution was signed and the Liberty Bell sits and they are named after the symbol of our great nation. I guess I'll let you decide that one!

Your mom has her own reasons for being a Saints fan. I think you'll have to ask her about that one. Although I don't know exactly where her fandom originated, I do know that her passion for her team and football was an exciting one of the many reasons I chose to marry her. If she didn't like football at all, it would have been a little different. For God's sake, your baby announcement was in football jerseys, I'm sure you'll see the pictures! Our wedding photos included, you guessed it, football. We brought our teams jerseys with us not too long ago to Disney's Magic Kingdom as an impromptu birthday getaway for Susana, knowing we might have to watch our games someplace close to Disney. Along with that, we (Susana will tell you that it was my idea) went to Magic Kingdom early in the morning just to take a priceless photo that we used to reveal your gender to the world! And yes, we were donning our Green and Gold!

So, the moral of this letter is that although you may not be a football fan, I hope you find some fun and passion in something. Actually, I hope you have a lot of things you are passionate about. You never know if one day that same passion will bring you closer with the person you love. I know for me, football was one of many connections that brought your mother and I together. I also believe that if you set out looking for new hobbies, adventures and set new goals you will be successful. You might not be good at something the first time around but if you give it just one more try, maybe it'll stick. Don't give up if you don't get the result you want. Part of life is learning from failure. If you lose, congratulate your opponent and understand a few things that you might have done better. However, don't dwell on it more than a day because tomorrow is a new day and another chance to do something great. Be great! You can accomplish anything in life if you're willing to work for it.

I love you Carson, Go Eagles!

15 OCTOBER 2018

You never know what kind of day you're going to have. You wake up everyday and look around wondering what the world might have in store for you. Where does your mind go? Do you think about the day before or look at the day ahead? Do you wonder where you are? If you are anything like me, you'll have a few of those!

Well today is a crappy day. Your mom and I are fighting as we tend to do from time to time. The fights are usually started by arguments that seem to carry over to the next day. We are both very stubborn and don't like to give in or concede to the other. We have not talked all day and even while I sit here writing to you I feel I miss her yet, I don't want to be around her. I am letting the *whatever* feelings to myself as she most likely is as well. The sad part is I even stopped at McDonald's on the way home to get her a few of the items I know she likes. Cheeseburger, no onions, 10-piece nuggets, medium fries and NO sauce. I quietly went into the bedroom where she was when I got home and put the bag of treats on the bed for her and simply walked out. I knew there was still an issue because if she was in the family room watching TV as usual, that would have meant she wanted to chat or talk things over. Arguments and fights suck. You feel like you are missing a part of you. Your mother and I are good at arguing and getting upset at each other. It makes me nervous because I don't want you to ever think that we are arguing because of you.

Driving home today, I was thinking about being a good dad. Not just a good dad, but a GREAT dad. I want to be in your life as much as possible. I want to make sure I set the example of what a good person, son, brother, husband and father can be. I am far from perfect. I promise you, your mom will be able to talk to you for hours on that subject. I have made a lot of mistakes and taken dumb risks. I have hurt people and I have lied. There are things that I have done that I am probably not aware of, so sometimes that feeling takes over and will make you hope that you can one day make it right. Usually gloomy, sad days will bring out the feelings that you put away on a regular basis. You'll do your best to always put on a smile, roll up your sleeves and make every effort to be the best you can be. However, it is inevitable that bad days will happen and they usually involve multiple things. They say bad things come in threes. Well, it might even be fours, fives and sixes! Don't worry, you'll get through it.

It's okay to be sad and it's okay to need to have times you just need to be left alone. Use that time to reflect or do something creative or distracting. I was by no means in the mood to write to you today, but I felt that maybe through the darkness I was feeling, I'd somehow put the words on paper and be able to somehow get a message out to you. In a way, it will be a way for me to have a little happiness in my life.

I promise to make every effort to be a good husband and good father. I want you to always be able to take my hand, literally and hypothetically, knowing that you'll always be safe. I owe everything I have to my parents. They stayed together over the years and raised a pretty good kid. That kid made some mistakes. That kid did some dumb things, but I always knew the worst part of screwing up was that I let me parents down. It was hard knowing that I upset the two people that gave me a chance, that showed me that I could be something special and that hard work would one day pay off. My goal is to lead by example, try to instill a good moral character in you so that you will be able to learn for yourself. If you ever think that something you are doing might disappoint your mother or myself, then let that sink in.

Sometimes you'll have moments that stick with you for a lifetime and the only way to ever get a feeling of comfort will be to own up to it, apologize or talk about it with the one you love. I did that a few times with both my mom and dad. I have also come to find out that sometimes I yell or get upset with people. I have done it in the past and I still do it now. Although it is a difficult reaction that I have always struggled with, I know deep down that if I didn't get emotional then it meant I really didn't care.

I can admit that I have struggled with a few emotional disorders over the last 6-10 years and unfortunately, I am still seeking treatment and trying to find peace. This is not to say I do not have ambition, drive or motivation. I simply have a condition that I am aware of and cannot always control my anxiety. It causes me a lot of undo stress and tends to show its ugly face at the worst times. I may go into it more as the letters progress. I just know that I need to be honest with myself as well as other people. Tomorrow I will be going to the VA hospital where I have gone off and on again for over 8 years to try and find a solution for my strange and difficult to deal with mood disorder. This is by no means a pity party. I am just putting my thoughts to paper. My emotions and anxiety disorder have ruined relationships and made others difficult to maintain. I have not been able to find a solution through therapy or prescriptions. I am going to fight really hard to get myself as mentally healthy as possible because I owe that to you and your mom. You deserve my absolute best. I guess you can say this is sort of my pledge to you.

I think knowing that I am going to be a dad has made me realize that I had a pretty good one myself. My dad impressed me in so many ways. I know for a fact that many things he taught me I use today. Confidence, holding my head up and working hard were some of the biggest traits he instilled in me. I want to be the dad that you look up to. Lucky for you I am six foot one so you have plenty of time to do that!

More importantly, I want to be your hero.

I love you, son.

15 DECEMBER 2018

I took nearly 2 months off. It stinks because when I first started writing to you, my goal was to write to you every day. It shouldn't be *that* hard right? Wrong. Life has this crazy way of just pushing and pulling you in all directions and it can be very time consuming. Your father had the bright idea to continue his education and go for a Master's Degree in Acquisition and Contract Management from the Florida Institute of Technology! Sounds great, but try and work that into an already pretty busy schedule that involves 10 to 12 hour workdays with commutes, a home to take care of, along with a beautiful and always glowingly happy, pleasant wife! Not to mention, we love to have plans all the time doing a bunch of fun things with friends and just exploring on our own. The good news is, the first semester went great! I made out with an A and an A+. No big deal! I plan on using this degree to get myself into the government contracting career field. It would be a nice challenge and will certainly be rewarding. So, we'll see how it goes!

I guess I'll sum up the last 2 months so you don't feel like I left you out of the loop. Sienna, our oldest dog, had her first seizure. It was sad and very scary because she's been with me through a lot. She is 11. I was very worried because I thought that she might have had a much more serious problem. After a morning at the vet, multiple exams and tests and a very hefty vet bill, it turns out Sienna just wanted to spend some quality bonding time with me and go for a car ride. Nobody could seem to find anything wrong. Go figure. However, through that fiasco, it made me realize that time is always fleeting and there will be moments that you'll never get back. Time doesn't wait or give you second chances all the time. So, this situation reemphasized how important it is to make every moment count. Spend a little extra time with your dog, friends, family, etc. You might not always have them around. Make their lives special even if it's for a few minutes. I took Sienna on a short peaceful walk like we used to almost every day. Since we have a larger yard those walks and trips to the dog park haven't happened nearly as much as they used to.

In the last few months we also had a few really special holidays. First, Veterans' Day and the Marine Corps birthday happened early in November. Obviously, your mother and I hold those two days very close to our hearts. As Marines, we always honor our fellow brothers and sisters that we served with along with all the other Marines that served before and after us. We make it a special point to remember the ones we lost along the way and especially those that sacrificed everything in battle. I tend to have recurring dreams, and nightmares if you want to call them that all around the months of September through November. I know deep down that there was a lot of anxiety about trying to get out of Iraq and home in one piece early in my military career. I think the thought and constant reminder of military personnel (which is a badass thing) around that time of year heightens my senses and memory receptors.

I looked at and read a portion of my journal that I kept in Iraq from 2006-2006 in Fallujah. I have always had the idea that I would one day edit it and get it published. I believe that I want to have it down on paper and saved so that maybe one day somebody will understand what I've done and what I went through. Plus, maybe you will want to read it and share that story with your kids. I love history documentaries and writings. I think once you're old enough to read this compilation of letters, you'll be able to read about your dad in combat. I also have a feeling that for the first 10 years (I can already hear your mom saying 15 years), I will probably have to read this to you and leave some parts out. Basically, I am going to include my journal in these letters to you. I want you to one day realize the importance of our military and the sacrifice of some of the heroes that don't make it back. I am so grateful to be here and I honestly believe I defied the odds to be able to sit here in our wonderful house married to a beautiful woman waiting for our first baby. It goes way beyond just making it though a few tours in Iraq.

Thanksgiving was special this year because we are grateful for all the things we have in our lives. As I mentioned before, friends, family, a nice home and yes, you are on the way! It is important to look around, not just on Thanksgiving but on any occasion to remind yourself that everything is alright. You have a pretty darn good life. It could always be worse. Just think about that once in a while. I promise there are many people who can't say it'll be alright. There are plenty of people with far less means, no home, food, or clean water that at the end of the day still can say they are at peace and it'll be okay.

A final thing that has been one of the most exciting things for me has been feeling you kick and wiggle around. It makes it so real and I honestly feel such a connection with you when I am able to feel you push a hand or foot against your mom's belly. She has been a champ throughout the pregnancy and I know I drive her off the walls crazy at times. We went to the Tran Siberian Orchestra at the Amway Center last night and apparently you really enjoyed that. You were moving around to the loud music outside her belly! I want to play some music for you while you're in there hanging out, waiting to come meet us. I think it'll do you good! I always say if I was forced to go live for a year on Mars I would need only a few things other than the basic food, water and shelter. One of those things is a huge music library. The other would be a way to record my days, my observations and my thoughts. Not bad, right! I love you, kiddo. Can't wait to finally see you. Final trimester is almost upon us!

20 DECEMBER 2018

Today, I am finally including the typed version of my Iraq Journal that I kept while on a seven-month tour in Fallujah, Iraq 2006. Please understand this journal was written in a hostile war zone that at the time was the most dangerous place on earth. I wrote in my journal when I felt safe enough to do so. This included writing using a red lens flashlight or headlamp flashlight so that other members of my rifle squad could sleep and not be bothered. Lastly, I use very raw language in *this* journal. I am sorry in advance!

Love you, Kiddo!

Iraq Journal

Lance Corporal Jon Olbrych
Started Saturday March 25 2006 15:23 MT

"Is it that while your life was easy, I walked along your side; but here, where the walking was hard and the path was difficult, the times you needed me most, those, my son, those are the times in which I carried you."
—Footprints

"I loved every firefight I was in because for those brief seconds nothing else mattered. It all comes down to the fact that you are going to die if you don't kill this guy and that's it…And all I have to do is live."
—What was asked of us, J. Olbrych

15:34 25 MARCH 2006

Today we left California (Twenty-Nine Palms) at 12:30. The temperature was in the 80s and it felt hot. We took a 2-hour bus ride to a nearby airfield, where we waited until 21:15 to take off towards our first stop: Bangor, Maine. (Basically 8 hours of sitting around eating, making calls home, and smoking, because everyone's nerves were on edge.) Anxiety was the keyword. It was a 6-hour flight to Bangor and we got an hour to walk around the airport. Out of maybe 350 Marines, about 100, including myself, ran out for a smoke. Bangor itself was pretty small and crappy. It had nothing but a military memorial room and some chairs to sit on. Next, we were on our way to Shannon, Ireland. This time, the reaction was very different; about 300 of the Marines ran to get in line at the one bar in the airport. Everyone had their token Guinness in Ireland. The Shannon Airport was pretty nice; it was much bigger than the one in Bangor and even had some stores.

We landed in Ireland at about 17:00 local time and the journey has already been about 14 hours long. Now here I am on another plane and it's 15:34 CA time, but I'm not changing my watch till I figure out where the hell I am! The flight attendant just said we have an hour until we hit Kuwait, so we'll see how all that goes in my next entry. Camp Victory (and a day of sure hecticness, but hopefully an opportunity to catch up on some rest…) here I come.

17:53 (KUWAIT TIME)
SUNDAY 26 MARCH 2006

Well, now I'm at Camp Victory. It's pretty big. We rolled in at 4:30, Kuwait time. I didn't stop looking out the window, just watching for anything I could see while I played country music to keep myself relaxed. Once here, we immediately got briefed on the Rules of Engagement (ROEs) and the rules of Camp Victory. We got ammo. Chow was maybe the best I've had in the Marine Corps: eggs, bacon, hash browns, even a bowl of Cinnamon Toast Crunch! Jet lag has kicked in. I got back from dinner 10 minutes ago and will probably sleep for a while. I've been sleeping since then, as have the other Marines. Rumor has it that we're leavin' at midnight for Iraq and we will be on base in Fallujah by tomorrow afternoon.

22:02 MONDAY 3 MARCH 2006

Well, today was another relaxing day. We're still at Camp Victory. I took 2 five-hour naps during the day and watched *Boiler Room* for the first time. The chow today was good. Nothing too different from yesterday. However, it did start pouring down rain about 2 hours ago. I've never seen bigger lightning in my life. It reaches across the whole desert. I just got back from the USO, where they have movies and couches that anyone can use; it's a pretty nice place! I guess they can't fly us out tonight, so rumor has it we're flying tomorrow night instead. All in all, I'm doing well and making the best of the "rest days." Keep the days counting **down!!!!**

06:44 WEDNESDAY
29 MARCH 2006

Now in my 4th country in a week, I am in a tent at the Al-Taqaddum Air Base in Central Iraq. We arrived here at approximately 04:00. We flew in on the C-130 and it may have been the ride of my life. We sat knee to knee in the pitch black, with legs interlocked, and then we dropped about 30,000ft in less than 5 minutes. The changes in air pressure definitely did a number on the head. The ride was loud, even with earplugs in. Once we hit the ground, everyone turned their game faces on really quick. Nervousness was everywhere and Marines were holding their weapons closer than I've seen so far this activation. I was in the same boat, especially being the 3rd man off the back-loading plank. Now that we're here and can see…it's not so bad. We were in full combat gear with ammunition for the landing but now we don't need all of that on base. It's pretty secure (security is by far a lot stricter than at Camp Victory). Plus, the food is just as good as in Kuwait! I'm lying here with my country music on to calm down and waiting for our first combat patrol to the CMOC (slums of Fallujah, our firm base) that is taking place tonight at approximately 22:00. So now I am going to get some sleep, then check out the new area. It has a new crappy smell. Flying in, we saw troops lined up in long formations outside, looking to go home. I thought to myself, that'll be me in seven months and it'll be one of the happiest moments of my life.

07:32 FRIDAY
31 MARCH

I need to backtrack a little to two nights ago. We were all loaded up in these huge up-armored 7-tons at 03:30, ready to convoy to what is now Baharia, rather than our base in Fallujah. At approximately 04:00, the convoy was supposed to be "wheels rolling," since it as going to be light out. 3/7 and another company were supposed to act as security for us as we went through. They actually got word that we'd received a no-go order from our command, so they scratched their mission. Now at 05:00, we were told that we were going through anyway. The route we were taking had several small arms attacks and two attacks from Vehicle-Borne Improvised Explosive Devices (VBIEDs) in the past few weeks. We were briefed to expect contact and to be ready for anything. Everyone's attitude at this point was "we're gonna get massacred," since we basically had no protection and we were moving during the daytime. They even called the General to see if they could push us through anyway. Well the convoy got cancelled. Thank God. So yesterday was another day of waiting around.

Last night, we did our first convoy into Fallujah (and it was intense for our first one!) We went right through downtown Fallujah on our way to where we are now (Baharia).

Fallujah is a shithole. We basically fucked everything up in OIF I and II, but it's still cool to see. Nobody is allowed out at night because of a mandatory curfew from 22:00-04:00. Last night, I slept pretty well, except for being 20 minutes from the center of Fallujah and hearing about 6 mortar rounds go off in our area. Anyway, Baharia is the nicest looking base yet. There are small ponds with bridges and palm trees. This is the site of Ude Hussein's palace, which we turned into a Marine base after blowing the crap out of it. The palace is on a little island that was totally demolished. It's not bad but we're closer to the action than ever. However, we're here for 2-3 more days until we travel in small 12-man convoys to our firm base at the CMOC in downtown Fallujah. So far so good. P.S., the living space is 12 men crammed into a room the size of my room at home; it's cramped!!

20:35 SATURDAY
1 APRIL 2006

I'm sitting here waiting for our convoy time, which is still up in the air. The sea bags are packed and the gear is all ready to go. For the last 2 hours, there have been constant mortar rounds going off in the Fallujah area. All of our platoon has been standing outside, watching and hearing the bangs in the distance. I know people are worried because everyone is loading up extra ammo from wherever we could get it. Somehow, we were able to get plastic bags with loose ammo. The mindset just changed drastically and people are listening to pump up music and drinking energy drinks. When a mortar goes off, luminary rounds (signals that light up the sky and look like fireworks) go up. The scary part of that is that the red signal means contact or Quick Reaction Force (QRF) is needed and shit is going down. Red signals mean Troops in Contact (TIC) We think that rumors got around that the change (Relief in Place) is happening and the insurgents supposedly realize all the movement in the area. Let's just say everyone is a little on edge. I know I am. Nobody knows what we're about to drive into.

21:05 SUNDAY 2 APRIL 2006

Ok, so we did our convoy last night, making it into the CMOC. It went well, with no contact. We were all on edge and screaming out anything we saw that looked suspicious, from wires hanging down to holes in the road. Once we got all of our packs and sea bags up to the rooms, we tried to get the lay of the land. It was a four-story building like an old rundown apartment complex and the walls on the outside were made of sandbags. There was a large generator in the front, covered by sandbags and a fuel pod that held fuel for generators and our small motor pool. I saw maybe 10 Humvees of all different colors. Some were high backs that you can fit 6-8 guys in and others were green, tan or a mix of the two. We got settled by 04:00. It was shitty, dirty, and there was mud pretty much everywhere you could see outside. There were sheets of cut plywood laid down to make a path leading in and out of the building so no one was walking through 4-6 inches of mud and water. Apparently, this was the end of the rainy season.

We wear full gear everywhere except when inside our rooms, where we have to have our rifles and flak jackets within arm's reach. It was all good until my squad of 4 got called along with 8 others and were told that we would be leaving on another convoy back to the place we had just come from due to the recent contact we'd been taking. By 14:00 we got our brief of where we were going and some of our tasks. This was a pretty crazy convoy due to the fact that the first daytime convoy had been hit by an IED and had a squad that had captured the trigger man.

This was my first daytime convoy. Every vehicle or person we passed seemed to be giving us crazy looks. This kind of messed with us, because we were told months ago to shoot anyone who looked or acted threatening or was seen "observing troop movement." We didn't engage because EVERYONE looked hostile! We made it safe back to Baharia 20 minutes (45 minutes convoy time) outside of the CMOC that was located in the dead center of Fallujah. We'll spend the night here, then my team, along with the others, will be outside Fallujah. We will be manning a Vehicle Check Point (VCP)/Entry Control Point (ECP) on the outskirts of the city. We're pissed because we've been taken away from the main body. The ECPs are apparently no joke and we will be detaining people and possibly engaging in some firefights. The ECPs are a lot more vulnerable because they have fewer people and less security. Plus, supporting units are a short drive away. I am not too nervous, though.. They said we will be overseeing the Iraqi Army (IA) and Iraqi Police (IP) to make sure they are doing proper searches and are large presence at the points of entry into the city. It's a pretty intense task because these ECPs are how the small arms, rockets, and bombs get into the city. This will be for anywhere from 45 to 60 days.

10:22 WEDNESDAY
5 APRIL 2006

First of all, Happy Birthday! I knew that this birthday was going to be different. We just had the whole ECP get lined up because an Iraqi felt we had stolen money when we searched them. This meant that every high-ranking Officer was here. I have been the main Radio Operator for the last 12 hours. I was never really good at that but the SSGT here complimented me and said I'm the most efficient person he's had in a while.

Let me back up. We arrived at ECP-2 and got put right on post. I was the supervisor of the Vehicle Check Point (VCP) and I had about 6 Iraqi Police (IPs) and 10 (Iraqi Army *soldiers)* IAs under my charge and watch. Basically, I had to make sure they were searching the vehicles the right way. If not, I would pull them aside and show them what to do and what they missed. I made a friend, Ali, who had an MP3 player that has 50 Cent's "In Da Club," which had the line "it's your birthday." He would keep repeating those same few lines for the entire song when he sang along. I've heard him saying English words like bitches, hoes and mother fucker. He tells the others this and it's amusing to me because they have no fucking clue. He can understand a little of what I say and I am the same way with his Arabic. I've learned a few basic terms.

The vehicles we have to search are all shitty and falling apart. So far at this ECP, we have found and detained two possible insurgents. This place is another shithole, with 1 shower and 1 taped-together satellite phone that we can't really use, since we're always in River City. When something bad happens, like a casualty in the area or when a major operation is taking place, we sleep in what seems to be some type of renovated or taken-over funeral home. It's next to a large cemetery. There is a small prison gym with weights and equipment that were made by Marines. For example, weights made from cement in two coffee cans attached to a metal or wood pole. Other than that, this place sucks.

I am listening to a meeting right now and it sounds like we're going to be stuck at this place for almost the whole time. I know that if I tell my boys, they'll die. This place sucks and there is so much going on with very little sleep. I'm finally getting 12 hours off after this. The 2/6 guys are leaving today and that's a downer for our guys. Mail may come once a week if we're lucky. Who knows when we'll be able to purchase things for resupply, like small items and cigarettes. It looks like we got the short end of the stick and there is going to be little time off and a shitload of threats and possibilities of attack from inside Fallujah or from somebody trying to get into the city.

As long as I stay tough and strong this whole time, I am coming home. I can't trust the IPs and IAs. My boys have to be on their game since this is one of the worst posts possible. The heat will suck, but it will dry up all the mud. We need to get the ACs fixed, but who knows when that'll happen. It could be a long time.

07:36 SUNDAY 9
APRIL 2006

Well, I haven't written in a few days because it has been quite busy. Yesterday was filled with a 7-hour shift at the VCP, then a 4.5-hour shift at the South Tower post. It's a lonely, one-man post on the south end of our tiny, 2-acre compound that watches one of the main supply routes into the city. We received mortar fire approximately 15 minutes ago and are trying to confirm the impact area outside the barriers to our ECP. The day went well, but it seems like we're just getting more tired and get less sleep because we have to get up early all the time for work that needs to get done or because of small arms fire in the vicinity. Last night at 04:30, we had some kind of attack to our south wall so everyone had to get up out of their rack and get gear on. We had no confirmation or eyes on the perpetrators.

Now I have to be up in an hour and a half to be on post for another 7-hour shift. I do get 12 hours off finally after that, so I am looking forward to showering and sleeping. I've been extra tired due to the food poisoning that hit me the other day. I threw up 4 times, once on post. I've had the tightest stomach cramps of my life and have had dizziness whenever I'm motionless and or sitting down. All is well now, I've got my stomach and strength back and will probably go back to working out later today.

Another ECP in another area of the city got hit by a VBIED about 10 minutes ago. There was a small firefight outside our ECP that lasted approximately 5 minutes that ended with no casualties. I'm pretty much just getting used to this way of life. Although this sucks, the days need to start just going by. The latest information I have heard was that our backup at the train station (about 5 miles east of us and within sight distance), Bravo Company, is pulling out in 2 months to go back to Camp Baharia. This will make us the last single standing post (ECP) outside of Fallujah. This makes our 25 guys much more vulnerable, since the insurgents will know that our support/quick reaction force (QRF) of 250 Marines is no longer that close. We will be getting a squad-size backup team (12 Marines) to be on-site with us. Who knows how that will go.

TUESDAY 11
APRIL 2006

Well, today is just a continuation from the day before. The long shifts are still the same, but now we're getting fucked in our off time, too. When we can get a full block of 6-8 hours of sleep, it ends up getting broken up into 3 periods of 2 hours each, since we have to do shit work to maintain the place. The 2nd shift is going on right now. Everyone is feeling this. People are saying that "jail is better than this!" They at least get sleep, TV, phones, visits, and food. Having only 25 guys to run this thing is almost stupid. If we do get sleep, we sleep with boots on, since we have to be the "react team." Still no fans or working AC yet. If we could have maybe 10 more guys out here, we could at least live almost comfortably and pull at least 8 hours off time for sleep or rest in a 24-hour period. We are getting a few close calls on bad guys each day. This is maybe the worst little 300 square yards in all of Iraq.

18:05 THURSDAY
13 APRIL 2006

Well, nothing new today. Yesterday was the closest I've been to a firefight, though. I went over to Bravo Company's Forward Operating Base (FOB) at the train station for an updated class on radio frequencies for the entire area of operations, including crypto (used to scramble our radio signals) and other classified shit. I went over with 2 others in a Hummer. The location is a few miles away, but you still never know what to expect. So, once we got there, a Gunny came out and gave us the class right there in their outside area. About 10 minutes into it, the FOB, which is an old blown up train station, took fire from the city side. I heard the rounds impacting a wall that was not more than 30 feet away. A squad of Marines came running out to set up. They did not fire right away, since they could not see who was firing at them. Then, sporadic fire of both insurgent and Marine machine gun fire went on in small intervals. Still, I could hear it only about 30 feet away from me. The engagement went on for a few minutes and ended with no casualties.

12:30 14 APRIL 2006

A few minutes ago, a Marine from Charlie Company took a gunshot to the leg, which I heard about over the "net." The initials are CA, last 4 are 2126, B+ blood type. That is all that was released and all they will say over the radio for identification purposes. Nobody else out here knows except me but the Marine sitting here with me. I also just got back from assisting a detainee to our holding cell. I was in charge of questioning him. He told us that he knows where bombs, RPGs, Mortars, and AK47s are buried. He asked us to keep him in holding and to keep him hidden, because he will get killed if anyone bad (Ali-Babas) see him as an informant to the Marines. He told us this because he lives with his wife and kids a block away from where they were hiding the weapons. He also said the "Ali-Babas" plan on digging up the weapons and attacking at night some time in the near future. This might be the greatest accomplishment for me so far this deployment. Right now, my mind is racing, plus I don't know who from our company got hit just now. So much shit is picking up right now. I wonder if they are saying anything on the news?

22:19 14 APRIL 2006

We just got back from a small arms & RPG attack on our compound. I was trying to fall asleep when it started. 1 marine came running in, yelling for everyone to get their shit on and get to their battle positions. SSgt took 150 rounds to the roof in all. 2 RPGs were shot. I put my boots on with no socks. Some guys didn't even put their trousers on. I had no shirt under my flak jacket. We shot up about 10 looms. They are 40mm grenades fired from a 203-grenade launcher attached to an m16 rifle. They light up a large area so we can see around us.

I led the charge of about 5 Marines out to the south wall where the fire had come from. I've never run so fast in my life while keeping my head down. I couldn't even tell if the rounds were still coming our way. I was yelling at the south tower with the machine gun (240B) to our 9 o'clock to tell us where the fire was coming from and to see if they could give us a location on the shooters. Nothing. They said it came from the building at our 2 o'clock, to the right of the bridge. I sat in a small bunker with Bautista with our M16s aimed out.

It went silent, other than Marines shouting to make sure everyone was okay and getting the "good to go" from every post. We sent extra bodies to the rooftop and to the rear gate. All hands scrambled everywhere. REMEMBER WE ONLY HAVE 25 guys until backup or until QRF comes from Bravo Company 2 miles away at the train station. They came with 20 or so Marines. Everything calmed down and we settled back in and gathered around a tiny movie screen and put in *King Kong* while we waited for the word that we could take off our gear.

What a rush…Expect more. Shit around here is getting rougher.

THURSDAY 20
APRIL 2006

Well, it's been a few days since I have written. Not too much has happened. In the city, there has been a daily IED explosion. 2 nights ago, we took some sniper fire. Each night has had some firefights in the distance between 9 and 10 p.m. It's becoming a normal thing. Guys don't jump out of bed anymore. They don't go running to see if we can get some shots in. It's just a part of the daily routine.

Another thing is the annoying prayer that bellows from the city. It happens 3-4 times a day that the chants of Islam are played in every mosque throughout Fallujah. It's just annoying chants and mumbles. Occasionally it sounds like a guy having a conversation with himself. Marines will often scream "SHUT THE FUCK UP" while on post because it seems like the awful noise will never end. It averages 30 minutes at a time.

Anyway, they are switching out all the beds with mattresses and changing them with military cots. This is because everyone but me and a few others has this rash all over their bodies. The Doc says it's probably bed bugs, so we will end up burning the mattresses in our burn pit. It's spread to almost everyone here and rumor has it that nobody else in the AO has it. Most guys' arms and legs look like they are covered in small chicken pox-like bumps. Either way, I'm pissed off because I like my mattress and the cots suck. Oh well, just another bull-shit Marine Corps thing I have to deal with!

SUNDAY 30 APRIL 2006

Yeah, it's been quite a while since I've written anything. 10 days to be exact! Things were hectic a week and a half ago and they sure haven't slowed down at all. One day we had the IPs and IAs basically shoot at each other with AKs that they pointed at each other's heads. This is never good, because US Marines work with them every day. So that day we acted as riot control. I was in charge of holding one of the instigators from the IA side. Man, was he pissed. I had to cuff him (we have zip ties for handcuffs) and had to watch him in our detainee room until we could figure everything out.

Other than that, I guess you could say we are just... here. Nothing really good, but nothing really bad, either. We get news on what's happening in the Area of Operations (AO) with our company and sometimes other parts of Iraq. It sucks, but can we talk about morale? What's morale? I think there are 2 types of morale while overseas in a combat zone. Morale overall is how you are feeling. An underlying feeling of how lonely and really miserable you are. I miss everyone and everything I left behind. On every post all we talk about is what we're going to do when we get home: life, school, HS, HS Sports, our girlfriends or wives. I mainly focus on what I'm going to do, my life goals, my life plans, my goals with school, money, job, work, etc. But at the same time, I'd go crazy talking about if I had millions of dollars and what I'd buy or where I'd go.

We even argue about the first thing we'll do when we get off the plane in the States and we're home for good. Do we stop for food (real, good American food) or will we be too excited to just get home and see our towns, our houses, our old lives? That's why morale in general sucks. All you have time to do out here is think and be on posts for hours and hours. We sweat our balls off and just talk about how lonely and shitty this place is. We don't worry about explosions in the distance anymore. That doesn't faze us. Gunfire isn't shit unless you actually hear them impact within 50 feet. This is how the days and nights go by. It's one continuous cycle. Somebody said the other day, "I just can't wait to sit on a porcelain shitter and be able to flush." It's the simple things like that that we are all down about. Each minute turns into hours, which turns into an entire shift or post of 6-10 hours. Then there's the sleep interrupted every hour because there is something wrong or there is an attack somewhere. It's a cycle that continuously fucks you up and there is no real motion. It's all scrambled together and time doesn't make sense. Morale - what a great thing...

Morale at ECP 2 in my mind is that everything will suck. I'm lonely and I miss everything. I have "my spot" out back where I go for a cigarette where I usually go in the mornings and at night. I just smoke, think, and listen to my country music with my earphones in. I even say a prayer every now and then. Since I adopted my spot, it kind of feels like it's my possession, just like my rack, my sea bags, the shared car packages under my bed and my pack.

I'm feeling a little more like "the man" out here. I seem to have a different connection with each of the guys we're with. A lot of the guys are calling me Jon. This is the first time I've been called that since I've been in the Marines because you always go by your last name. It's funny when you realize that you don't know somebody's first name, even though you've known them for years. So, in our little shithole I am actually doing alright as for the comradery with all the guys. But as crazy as this shit is, I sometimes need to get away and have some time for myself, since in our little free time everyone wants me to come work out, or watch a movie, or just smoke, talk, or do other stupid shit out here. Sometimes when I get off either a machine gun tower or the vehicle checkpoints, I just need sleep. But. I guess sometimes it's a good feeling, knowing people look to me for a morale boost. I've made friends with most people because they know that I'm dependable and have a pretty good attitude day to day. It's just that when I'm told to do shit, I don't bitch like some other people because it gives me something to do. Anything that takes up time is good. Time that goes by is time that is getting me closer to being home!

MONDAY 8 MAY 2006

So, I'm sitting here as yet another day is beginning. The last week has brought the same old bullshit. Sleep for minimum hours, get woken up for stupid shit, post on the checkpoint line for a long period of time, then a night post. So much is going on everywhere around us and we have been on constant alert for vehicle-borne bombs and cars that could be used to blow us up. We had female Marines one day show up to come and search women. They found over 9,000 US dollars on 2 women alone. They also found Syrian money taped to the stomach or one woman under her burka. This was way too much money for one person to have. This means that money for terrorism is still around.

Yesterday, I was the first one out to our personnel search and found that Iraqi civilians had broken the gate to enter the ECP and were on the bridge. That is a scary situation because we don't know if they planted an IED anywhere. We told the IAs to go tell every car on the bridge to turn around. They started rioting and it got heated to the point that the IAs had to use gunfire and start ramming cars back to get the situation under control.

The battle we are fighting is only getting crazier. Who knows if we are winning? I mean, we have already had multiple WIAs and 2 or 3 KIAs. It's sad and most of us get pissed off when we hear the news, but then we realize this is war and it's going to happen. Yet, I see half these guys thinking "thank God it's not me." So who knows, this place is by far the worst place in the world and if it's a "calm day" here at ECP-2, 30 other things happen 1-3 miles away.

MONDAY 15 MAY 2006

Well, bad news has come since the last entry. We had our Commanding Officer Captain Lauders killed by an IED. He was the one whose wife is in charge of the Marine Network for the families back home. The Marine Network keeps the families of all the Marines informed and in the loop as much as possible.

My original squad got hit by an attack and one member got shot straight through the neck. Thank God he survived and is going home in stable condition. The bullet went through at such a high velocity from the sniper rifle that it cauterized the entry and exit wound almost completely so he didn't bleed out. Barney is a good guy. He graduated from Harvard and has said he wants to get into politics and maybe even be President someday.

2 others got shot. One was really bad in the head, but he is miraculously somehow still alive and will be going home in stable condition. Someone was saying they're calling him "Lucky Link." There were a few other injuries with roadside bombs. Just yesterday, a terrorist cell tried to shut down our ECP and was blocking people from coming in. They put out an alert that they were going to send a large bomb through hidden inside a dump truck. It was a good thing we got the intel and were on high alert with extra over watch posts. We did get a small attack the other night with 2 RPG rounds

fired in the direction of our building and only made out 2 or 3 insurgent bodies fleeing. We had no confirmed kills even after we unloaded the 240-machine gun and all of us got to our designated QRF positions. But hey, everyone is fine and we repelled yet another enemy small arms attack. I just want to laugh at anyone who tried to reassure me that I would be on a ship like Des who left for boot camp the same day I did and that we wouldn't be in the action.

Tonight, I smoked out of a hookah with some of the guys and our interpreter who had this fine Arabian tobacco (NOT DRUGS!). We did get yelled at by SSgt, but we enjoyed it for a little while and took pictures, but then had to put it away, since SSgt said it was drug paraphernalia. But that's the news for now. I'm still stuck working long hours with no real sleep. We are all trying hard to stay sane. It's difficult, but I'm just trying to stay positive and I can tend to be pretty sarcastic at times. But hey, I'm just being me and somehow getting away with it. I do haircuts now and word got out that I do pretty decent ones, so I've done 22 total now. I should keep record and charge these guys when we get home since we obviously don't have cash out here.

SATURDAY 20
MAY 2006

So, the latest action was seen just yesterday. The IPs got ambushed on top of the north bridge at around 07:30. There were 3 RPGs fired at their vehicles and around 5 or 6 insurgents with a heavy barrage of AK47 fire. Our ECP took fire and the shots hit the barriers where our gym is. As usual, everything was crazy and we returned fire. We don't know if we killed anyone. The ReACT team showed up right around that time, so everything got disoriented. This was the longest firefight yet and it lasted about 15 minutes. The IPs on the bridge supposedly got so pinned down that they set down their AKs, sat down cross-legged, and surrendered (we'll see what that outcome of that is soon).

That was yesterday. Two days ago, a Marine went off on his own and walked into the desert or something after getting pissed off. There were patrols all night both on foot and by helicopter looking for this idiot. It was a big deal because he was more likely going to end up shot dead than found alive, either by enemy fire or shot by Marines for being a deserter. So, this stunt had the other Marines and I standing on our rooftop posts for an extra 3 hours looking for this moron. What is even better is that this was when I was finally going to have 8 hours off. If the insurgents didn't kill him I think I might! The latest I have heard is that my squad back in the shittiest part of the city has taken many attacks and had a few very close calls, including many more WIAs that had Marines with tour-ending injuries.

Fuck, I'm nervous. Who knows what can or will happen? I am close to my team and I know we will bring each other home safe. June 2nd is the date posted for us to head into the city. Rumor has it that it'll be for 12 days.

SUNDAY 21 MAY 2006

Well, today dragged on until we finally got off posts. I realized I haven't described yet this gross thing that we use out here. It's called the "wag bag" and we use it to take a shit. Yes, it's a mini portable plastic toilet seat. You place this small trash bag thing that has cat litter in it, do your thing and put it in this little biodegradable disposal bag that comes in the little pouch with it. I thought it would be something new to talk about and since we have to man posts for endless hours we have to make do with this kind of thing. Nobody can come relieve you since they all have to try and get at least some sleep.

Also, there is this fat lazy corporal who was pissing everybody off that I stood up to and made look like an ass. Today was just normal posts and stories we told to kill time. Lambert and I had post and told every funny story we could remember from high school all the way up to last summer. We talked about our girlfriends. We were dying laughing most of the time and we realized we are very similar, especially when it came to some of the bad things we did back in high school. My good friend Davidson made me a CD, since I somehow found a blank CD. I now have a rap CD! But it's good, party, club, drinking music. It's new and something different for a change.

So, I realized I can't do anything without anyone wanting to talk to me or throw a football with me when we are in our off time. Even last night, when I made my own little ash tray and wanted to smoke in my rack about 10 minutes later, I had 5 guys come over to hang out with me. I am realizing I must be a pretty cool guy. I'm not trying to be cocky, but everyone likes me. Even the other corporals and the SOG (sergeant of the guard). Only Corporal "fuck nuts" doesn't like me and doesn't realize I'm a pretty good guy. This place still sucks but we're "ripping" (being relieved in place by another group of 25 or so Marines) out of here the 2nd (which means in Marine Corps time the 10th), which is fine with me. I just want to get this over with.

TUESDAY 23 MAY 2006

So, I just got back in from a firefight. Well, somewhat. Let's just say it was the closest I have come in my life to getting shot. Maybe 10 feet away, to be exact. I was at the post at our front gate as the Hummer came out. I heard the explosion just outside of the city. Then, what sounded like small arms fire ended up being 2 cracks (shots that impacted in the cement 10 ft tall Texas barrier about 20 feet away from me). I froze in place and blocked the road. Cpl Burnes looked at me like I was stupid when I signaled for them to stop immediately.

I immediately closed the gate and blocked them from heading out into the area taking fire (they may have been pop shots or possibly sniper fire). I saw a round go into the dirt to the right of me and another one made a whizzing noise. I ran to the side of the Hummer for cover and yelled that we are taking fire. Burke opened the door as more shots went by and screamed something about going to the South Tower. I ran to the cement wall and yelled into the radio for Davidson (at South Tower) to fire. He opened up with the 240 as I looked for shooters in the field. Nothing at first, but then I saw guys armed with rifles (about 200-300 meters out) and fired. They ducked down behind a berm (huge sand mound) and I didn't see them again. Everything came down.

A Major came running over and asked me to describe the situation and let him know where all the Marines were, such as posts and after-action briefing. He commended me and said we did an awesome job but at the same time "CALM DOWN, BREATH!!" I had too much adrenaline pumping through me at that time. So that was today's excitement. We also brought in one of the highest-ranking terrorist members of a large terrorist cell out here. He had many fake IDs, $3,000 cash, and a handgun. This was a bad dude who was one of our High Value Targets (HVTs) and was wanted by the FBI/CIA. ECP-2 is being noticed and recognized as one of the best and most active checkpoints in the Al-Anbar Province.

SUNDAY 28 MAY 2006

Our north bridge took an IED explosion yesterday. From what we saw, a number of civilians and 2 Marines were injured and 2 IAs dead or injured severely. Also, one of my closest friends Davidson went down with a heat casualty. He's fine now. I was pissed that they made him stay on post for 9 hours until 12 noon. We even have a thermometer that said it was 109 degrees when he went down. The highest I've seen recorded has been 112. Last night brought some drama. The asshole corporals Mathews and Perez were drinking some whiskey that Perry stole out of a car at the Vehicle Check Point. I was pissed because as "leaders" they should not be hammered when you know at any minute we could get attacked. They also started fucking around wrestling or something and somehow a condition 1 (loaded with round in the chamber) pistol was brought out. I lost it. There is no way any of my guys or I are going home in a box because some fuckups accidently shot a round while fucking around.

So, I explained what had happened to the Corporal of the Guard and SSgt. They barely gave a shit. A bunch of my guys said they would back me up and write out paperwork saying what happened. I was just pissed because who was going to tell me where we should go and what posts to back up if we took fire? So, I knew I'd be in charge. I already have more sense than they do, anyway. Fuck those guys. The word on the street is they want to "fuck me up" but they are 2 big pudgy assholes. Plus, I know everyone else out here would back me up. Nobody likes their cocky, lazy, and unprofessional asses anyway. Out here, everyone helps out with everything except for those two lazy assholes. Well, either way, 4 more days at ECP-2 and we will begin ripping out of here. Hell hole number 2, here I come.

MONDAY 29 MAY 2006

Today at approximately 08:15, there was a huge explosion on our north bridge at Jundis (IA) and IPs went to open the ECP. It was followed by a large amount of gunfire. Let's put it this way: today will be a day that I will remember for the rest of my life and I'll leave this story out of my letters home. As the IED went off, it shook our over watchtower about 200 yards away. We looked around frantically and got behind our weapons (Lambert) was behind the saw light machine gun and I searched with my ACOG scope on my M16). As a looked in my scope, I only saw worse things. Not only was there sustained gunfire and IA/IPs firing from different positions, but I saw IAs going down. With my scope, it looked like they were only 400 meters away. I was screaming for someone to get back up teams out there, but since everything was so confused and in chaos, it really wasn't helping. Lambert and I had the worst seats in the house, other than the guys on the bridge.

My first reaction was to pop a red signal flare that indicates we are taking fire to get QRF to respond as a backup. We put up about 3 or 4 flares so that Bravo Co. (2 miles away) could send their QRF team. I will never forget the view I had or screaming at all the IAs to get out to the firefight. Next, an IA who was one of my buddies (a younger kid) was so panicked that he took the gun truck and drove it into the berm and just stared at me for a few seconds because he was terrified. I yelled for him to keep moving and grab one of the other trucks. The first truck that came back had the first casualty in its bed. I ran down when one of the IA limped over to the base of our tower with gunshot wounds to the arm and leg. He was bleeding heavily. I keep a tourniquet on my right shoulder at all times, so I used it and applied it to his arm to stop the bleeding. It was a pretty sickening sight. Afterwards, there were enough people responding to help with the casualties that I got back to my tower and watched as more IAs were getting shot. The next truck that came back from the bridge had an IA in the back who was saturated in blood. It looked like he took shrapnel to his femoral artery and many other parts of his vital areas, along with gunshot wounds. He was carried out of the truck by about 4 guys, but he was limp and going into shock.

Finally, about 30 minutes later, the QRF force from Bravo Co. showed up and headed towards the bridge. As they headed north on the sand road, a flatbed IA truck returned but did not stop this time. It rolled by our tower and went to the rear part of our ECP away from our casualty collection point (CCP). In the back were bodies that were missing arms or were all mangled up in most of the lower parts of their bodies. There was one with the right side was all torn up. In the back was another IA body that was missing 2 legs. The bloody, ripped up body that looked like hamburger meat will be something I don't know if I'll be able to ever forget. The 2 that were injured and made it back to our tower were put into the ambulance. We later found out that one of them later died in the ambulance. All that was left was a pool of blood where his body was on the pavement.

There were 3 or 4 IP trucks and about 4 IA trucks that were patrolling the area after the fighting stopped. We just sat there, wishing we could have helped, but we were just too far out of range to do anything. We didn't even really see anything except for some muzzle flashes on the other side of the bridge. I felt pretty sick. I wanted to cry as I saw each gun truck come back with bullet holes, broken windows, and blood from the injured. There were IAs and IPs that ran on foot over the sand mounds to get help. It was a sad day. There were many of them I consider friends and see every day. The hardest part was watching them hit the ground. Our fucked-up command was telling us to sit tight and hold our position until the reaction team got there. Next, they wanted to open the ECP to show that we still were strong and operational, but FUCK THAT. These guys sit in their AC computer rooms and will never see the pain and blood that the IAs, IPs and our Marines face each day. In the end, there were 4 dead (KIA) and 2 IAs that were badly injured. One, (Abu Surwah) lost his hearing and had his eardrums burst while bleeding from the ears. To me, it's just a realization that this is Iraq. It's war and I hope to God that all of us stay safe. This was a sad day..

(119 DAYS LEFT)
3 JUNE 2006

Today, I feel like a complete ass. I don't know what has come over me. Maybe it's because of all the crap food we have been eating. I haven't been eating right in general. I guess they didn't bring dinner or breakfast for us in the last day or so. The day before, I was eating half rations because the food is so shitty. I can make all the cup noodles and Easy Mac I want, but even that shit starts tasting bad after a while, especially when it's all you have. The AC is acting up and it's not even cool inside here anymore. I wake up soaking in sweat and that sucks. I have been drinking a ton of water.

I haven't really received any mail recently. I don't need any more packages, because most of the things people get, they leave out for everyone else to use. We have shitloads of everything, like baby wipes, sanitizer, and bug spray, which is nice. I haven't left like I thought I would. The first 3 guys left today. Our battalion did a huge raid all through the night until noon today. The mission was to take out a small terrorist cell that is responsible for the IED attack the other day and numerous other attacks in the last two weeks. I have been writing a lot of letters but it pisses me off because I get the feeling that nobody is getting them. It sucks, because the letters barely describe half of what we are going through out here. My buddy Lambert left to reunite with his squad back at the CMOC today. I think I should be going in the next 3 days. It's just messed up today because the focus is on the battalion attack. It's getting fucking hot. Each day is a little hotter than the last, I would guess around 120 degrees. Damn, it's hot! I'm getting a little tired of this shit! Well, maybe today is just one of those days, I guess everyone has them.

SUNDAY 4 JUNE 2006

So last night, four Marines showed up to start getting us ready to get out of here. I can't wait! This place sucks. Last night, half the power went out, so we only had half of our ACs or fans working. Awesome! It's bad. The only good news is that a Major came on deck and told us that as of June 1st 1/24 is officially activated and has started getting ready to come out here. Yesterday, there was also a 2-company-wide attack and raid mission right outside our ECP. The mission was to find weapons and some terrorist cells that attacked us the other day. From what we heard, it went smoothly.

I'm getting pissed off because we're getting neglected and getting leftovers from Bravo Company when we have to drive once a day just to get our warm meal from these huge green vats. I eat half rations anyway because if I eat a full plate I'll throw up. The last thing I'll bitch about is my fucking ankle. I don't know what I did, but when I took my boot off today, my left ankle was swollen to double or maybe three times its normal size. Its huge! The back of the ankle is sore, and the whole side is black and blue. I don't know if I want to tell Doc or not. If I did, they'd move me all over the place. I'm sure I could suck it up. I don't know though. On the other hand, it could get worse. Who knows? At least there's only another month until we're at the halfway point, which will feel seriously good. The slope will finally be going down-hill! Thank God, now I just have to survive the CMOC.

FRIDAY 9 JUNE 2006

Al-Zarqawi is DEAD. Last night, they confirmed that the #2 most-wanted guy in the world is dead and was killed in a Marine Corps air raid. The big joke now had been, "well now that he's gone, can we go home yet?" This last week has been shaky. I've been lonelier and more upset than usual. I've found myself not eating as well as I should. At the same time, I feel like it's their fault for giving us the same crappy old food and half rations. Crappy lettuce that's supposed to be like salad and some mystery meat is supposed to cut it for dinner? There was one day I was so sick of this shit that I just wanted to stay in bed. Yesterday, things got a little better when I realized on post that today is the 9th. I don't know, but it feels like maybe this month is going by a little faster. I don't want to say that aloud, though, because I know I'll just jinx myself.

Last night, there was a raid outside our compound. Nothing too special. I was told over a week ago that I would be out of here by now. I have most of my crap packed but "they" keep holding out and not telling me anything. Rumors are floating around that it'll be another week. I think the 20th of this month is the official half-way point, so at least that will feel good. It will be a countdown rather than a count up. I just want to get out of here. I've seen the same old shit every day. It's definitely getting old. I enjoy my role and have learned a lot, but I don't like getting told things only to then have people not really know what they're talking about. It's really awful, shitty communication. But hey, it's the Marine Corps…

FRIDAY 16 JUNE 2006

I don't even know where to start…Maybe with that in 2 hours, we will be rappelling into sewers and ravines on the outskirts of the city in search of a submerged weapons cache. Or how about that I got back from a patrol through the shittiest, smelliest, narrowest, most claustrophobic, scariest, shadiest, most blown-up, most torn-down, most run-down shanty part of the world I've ever seen. Or how about that the new CMOC (where I am now) was hit with a large mortar yesterday that destroyed 8 Humvee tires and 4 conex boxes outside our building, including our fuel pod. It was engulfed in flames and we lost a lot of our critical infrastructure. Oh, and today an engineer who was with us attached to an EOD unit was sniped in the face. Probably by the same sniper who shot another Marine in the arm yesterday.

In the days leading up to this, I was still at the ECP. I slept only 4 hours the day before I came out here. A part of me was sad to be leaving the jail that I called home for the first 2 and a half months of my deployment. The rest of me was nervous to see what lay ahead of me. It's sad to be leaving my IAs and IPs who knew me by name and it's a whole different world in the heart of the city. The slums are like pictures out of adoption ads. The kids come running, waving to me screaming for candy or a "football." Everyone is just standing around aimlessly with what looks like no care in the world. When we get out of the Humvees in the middle of town, they all just stare at us. They look scared, but at the same time, they seem like they want to try and talk to us and to ask us why we are here. We make cars crash or back up into other cars when we are driving down the roads and side streets. We have to take the side mirrors off on some of the Humvees because the roads and streets are way too narrow. The procedure for anyone that sees our convoy is for them to stop and pull over completely to the side of the road. People lock their brakes and get themselves injured because we will shoot if they come too close or look like a threat. We have Escalation of Force (EOF) procedures that mean we can wave a bright orange flag, throw a flash bang, or if necessary, fire shots at the ground to get them away from our convoy.

Tonight, there is going to be some crazy shit. The weather is still blazing hot and I don't really like my team leader, Cpl Fodry. He treats me like I don't know shit, but he's lazy and I don't see him being too great in a situation in which we take contact. I built a shelf in the room and started moving in. The room sleeps 4 and has a tiny AC unit with plywood and sandbags as our wall. Rumor has it that I may be sent out again to go on an MIT team. I'll explain that if it actually happens.

So much is going through my mind right now. I haven't been able to talk to anyone back home in a long time. We haven't even had mail in about 2 weeks. I know Kacey loves me, but I know that all this time apart is hard on her. Why should I do this to her? I don't want her thinking she can't have fun back home. She's working so hard with two jobs. It's probably so can keep her mind focused. Is the fact that I'm away holding her back? Maybe I'm losing my mind. I'm sure every guy out here with a girl back home has thought about this more than just once. Maybe it's just the loss of contact. I don't know how this is affecting my folks, either.

Hopefully it will all be over soon. I don't ever want to feel like this again. I don't want to have these crazy feelings or feel so far from home. Some of the things I see out here I don't ever want to have to see again.

MONDAY 19 JUNE 2006

Well, I'm doing fine. I got all settled in with my team in the CMOC. My boys Ivan and Chambo are with me from ECP-2. We're pretty close and always make fun of each other. I've been the driver on a few convoys already and have driven through some pretty shitty areas where anyone could pop out and shoot or place an IED. I'm still trying to learn the city. I'm sure it will come to me in time. I'm learning the key landmarks like the mosques, the graveyard, water towers, and the tiny amusement park in the middle of the city.

Last night was a night that I won't forget. I was sitting on the roof of our building with maybe 15 guys, a case of O'Doul's, and a box of cigars that Ivan's grandfather sent. We listened to Bruce Springsteen and a bunch of other patriotic songs. There was some Toby Kieth, the Taliban song, and some other American classics like "Born in the USA," the national anthem, and others. It was relaxing, but hilarious blasting the music overlooking the city of Fallujah. Posted on two of the corners were 2 snipers wearing sweatpants who had their rifles sighted on all of the buildings using their night scopes. I'm sure they had us covered if anyone tried to fire in our direction. The rest of us just sat there, listening to stories or lying down looking at the stars. 1stSgt calls this "Americantology." Apparently, this will be a weekly thing. Good times.

Our room is getting there. We built shelves with whatever we could find and replaced and refilled the sandbags that go in the wall, which was blown out by bombs at some point. There is a little mouse in there, but he's not bad. Then there's the city: what a fucking dump! The areas I've been to are terrible. It's sad to see people on their little slabs of cement, sweeping shitty sewage off into the tiny, unpaved streets. There's a tiny drain in the center that collects shit. The children are cute and little girls are actually beautiful. It's sad. We give out candy, soccer balls and some small stuffed animals from time to time, but recently stopped. There have been reports that the 6- to 10-year-olds have been throwing grenades at our patrols, so you can't trust anyone, not even the kids. It's a dirty war. There have been 9 or 10 grenade attacks so far this deployment. Tomorrow at 06:00, we are heading out to clear a section of the city. It has around 40 buildings and houses that intel has said are a hotbed for weapons caches, insurgents, and IED-making materials. Should be a blast!

WEDNESDAY 21
JUNE 2006

Today's raid and house-clearing went well. Objective A and B both went smoothly. I was the driver of the second Vic (vehicle). We were the cordon for the second operation. We moved up to the 3rd objective & set in. All of a sudden, a white Sidekick came right at us, cutting hard off of the main street onto the side street we were on. I took cover, along with a few others who were all on the outskirts of the cordon setting up for the mission. We threw a flash bang and then Mendez and I shot at the ground and into the grill of the vehicle. As my SAW let go, I fired a few bursts and opened up on the car, which was now 15 yards from us. Its tires locked up and it skidded to a stop, its front windshield shattered. I soon realized the driver had been hit and was slumped over the wheel. Once the vehicle stopped and the situation calmed down, we called for our corpsman. I assisted him in taking the driver out of the car and identifying his wounds. As we pulled the heavy set guy out (he was about 250-300lbs, about 50 years old), we saw a boy about 7 or 8 years old get out of the back passenger door, crying, and run across the street.

One thing I won't ever was the look on the boy's face. It was a mix of horrified, lost, and sad. I also won't ever forget the face of the man driving the vehicle when it stopped. He was gasping as his son tried to hold on to him. I don't know what the look on my face was like. It's just one more thing I wish I didn't have to see. Once we located the entrance wounds on the upper right of his ribcage, I knew it was not going to be good. The guy was bleeding, but not as much as I had seen before or expected, since he'd been shot a couple of times. He was breathing and after a few minutes he went into shock. We had to switch to providing security when a large group of curious people started gathering across the street. That's typical for whenever there's an explosion or gunfire. They're all curious people and now someone, one of their own, had been shot and was dying in the street.

An IP came over and I yelled for him to get one of the Bongo truck flatbeds so we could pick him up and try to get him to Camp Fallujah, which had surgical capabilities for major injuries. Once they got some civilians to help, I got back into VIC 2 to help the escort and haul ass to Fallujah surgical with the Bongo following. Once at Camp Fallujah, they told us that the man had died in the back of the truck on the way. He was processed and came out in a body bag about an hour later. Once we convoyed back to our firm base, I was told I would have to write some statements as a witness and a key person involved.

That took over an hour or so and afterwards, I finally got some down time. It's now Friday, June 23, go figure. I have been writing this entry in small segments between posts. Yesterday was a long day. I was in the company office at Camp Baharia because I was told I was being charged with theft and larceny. It was established that I was in the clear, but I was told I was a key witness. My statements were important because of some things that had happened while I was at ECP. There were two claims of racism and a case of drinking. There was also a charge of unfair treatment by the SNCOIC towards by friend O'Donnell. I spent 45 minutes answering questions and filling out statements in front of the SGAs (staff judge advocates) along with 2 others. It was a tough situation to be in, but I know I did what was right and was the best possible action for while we were in Iraq. I know I answered all of the questions honestly, although it was hard at times because I wanted the right things to be done.

After about 9 hours, we took a convoy to another ECP on another side of the city. I'm pissed that they did all this during a FUCKING WAR. Making a convoy for us to go write out statements and answer questions when there is a constant threat of attack that puts lives in danger is insane. I feel like there are far more important things that need to be done rather than putting Marines lives in danger. I gotta say, I've gotten right into the mix and have been on more convoys than a lot of people in the last two weeks. My experience is growing and I was actually the vehicle commander for the convoy yesterday. Usually that's the highest-ranking guy in the vehicle and I was it! I've been on post and have slept only 4 hours in the last 29 so, I'm at the point of wanting to pass out or cry! I'll be off post in 4 hours and I'll be off for 12..By then I'll be so tired I'll be able to sleep the whole time!

FRIDAY 30 JUNE 2006

Today, we did a patrol through the beautiful streets of Fallujah. It was a hike and I gotta say, my shoulders are hurting quite a bit. The temperature was worse than ever and it's freakin' hot. The 3rd patrol just got back and said it's up to 123 degrees and its only 1:45pm. I guess the good news is that it's the last day of this month. Most patrols are interesting, but this one was especially so. We went through the souk, which is a marketplace, and had pamphlets to hand out to people to tell them about this recruiting depot going on in a few days. The markets in this place are not normal at all. Imagine a place smelling like nasty burnt trash where people are selling their sinks, furniture, clothes, rugs, and food. Next to a produce stand of rotten food, you have goats and lambs getting slaughtered right there on the street corner. It definitely made me gag a little.

It's crazy the way all the people just stare at us. I guess it's understandable, because it'd be like a patrol marching through downtown or the mall or something back home. It's just scary because you don't know what they're thinking or if there is somebody in the crowd with a bomb vest on. There are so many little crevasses and dark areas hidden behind the stands that anyone could open up with gunfire or grab and pull a Marine through. A few people would actually smile and say salaam, but behind the smile they could be thinking, "I want these guys dead" or "these guys killed my family member years ago."

I guess I need to bitch about my "team leader" Cpl Jamison. I call him "the Jodster" to everyone else but him. He's the most annoying piece of shit, contradictory fat-ass around. He's the guy who's lazy, has no friends, and had absolutely no power or say in anything back home. But in the reserves while on drill and on deployment, he just loves the fact that he's an NCO and has one extra stripe. He has close to 6 years in the Marines and most people would made sergeant by then, but he probably just sucks at his PT score. He's always nagging you on patrols and trying to correct you, when he's the one who's actually wrong and is doing exactly what he is yelling at everyone else for. He's also one of those who starts yelling and making a scene whenever somebody important walks by in an effort to try to make himself look better or like he's some kind of combat genius. He always complains when he gets tasked with a more difficult mission. He's just a big, lazy, fat-ass clown! I have to deal with his shit for the next few months. At least I can finally see the light at the end of the tunnel. It's small, but it's there!

TUESDAY 4 JULY 2006

Well, I just got in from 2 hours of music and some really lame fireworks on the roof of the CMOC. I had my O'Doul's and smoked a cigar and a few cigarettes. It was somewhat sad and depressing, since we'd returned from a zone-clearing about an hour before and had taken fire from 2 different directions on our way in. It was probably IP being shot at in our vicinity, but we still had to move to cover. The joke was "well, there are your fireworks for the 4th!" I remember sitting in a courtyard with my team and saying, "happy 4th of July guys." We laughed and made a few comments on how this is the real meaning of the 4th of July. What could be better than this? Thinking back, I can think of over 20 things right off the top of my head. But hey, it's just another page of my life over with. It was depressing, sitting around in a room talking about all our previous 4th of July parties at home with friends and family. We heard some new rumors that may affect some of us. To the north is the city of Ramadi, which is in the Al-Anbar province like Fallujah. It's supposedly like the Wild West out there, like the first battle to take control of Fallujah, which lasted 20 days or so. This may affect me because they said they may send a unit into Al-Habbaniyah, a small section of the city that is pretty hostile, so we can have another angle on Ramadi. It's always something. We never get a fucking break! But I guess that's why we're Marines.

WEDNESDAY 5
JULY 2006

So today I had another near-death experience. Not 10 minutes before I was supposed to be prepping (pre-checking) my vehicle for our mobile patrol, 4 mortars fell outside our building. One hit just 5 feet from the main entrance and created shrapnel that exploded and even went through our sandbag-reinforce plywood walls. We ended up having 3-inch holes in our walls and splinters of wood falling on the ground. We ran to grab our gear to make sure we had all our guys. All good! The mission was still on, but delayed maybe 20 minutes. I went outside like I was supposed to in the first place. I was a little nervous, but I know from my previous experiences that they usually don't fire more than a few at once and never 2 mortar attacks in a row. Well, the vehicle that I was supposed to be driving (and prepping right around the time of the attack) got a direct hit. Not only did the mortar blow a hole through the steel roof, but the turret was no longer functional. The windows and doors were done for and the interior seats were all torn up as well. If I'd been out there before, I'd be dead. I took a bunch of pictures afterwards. I guess it was just another lucky day. Good thing God is on our side!

SUNDAY 9 JULY

As I sit here right now, I have to ask myself whether I appreciate my existence. What will I make of myself in the future? When will it finally be my time? I guess you should start thinking like this when you have 2 near-death experiences in 2 or 3 days. Honestly, I'm freaking myself out a little. How will anyone who reads this in the future feel?. Yesterday, I was called out on QRF for an IED cordon. Of course, everyone was a little pissed off because we had been out for 6 hours before this. So, my squad got into our vehicles and headed out to set up our cordon of the possible IED area. Cordons are set so that nobody can get in and usually nobody can get out unless they're in immediate danger. A cordon for a possible IED can take hours because there are so many found IEDs and not enough EOD (Explosive Ordnance Disposal) techs. Usually, we just hang out, looking for anything or anyone that looks suspicious until EOD arrives on the scene to blow it up or determine it's not actually an IED. They are known to not be very timely.

As we sat in our areas, scanning the road and the rooftops, Doc Greyson, who we all call Brock, and I were set in at the end of a side street on a small narrow road between the main road Fran and the cemetery. 30 minutes went by and nothing really was going on. We heard and saw a few kids' voices in a room on the second floor of a building near the end of the street. We saw this bike with 2 kids riding on it, one of them standing on pegs on the back, go by slowly, just sort of checking us out, since they were surprised we were there. A few minutes went by and out of the corner of my eye, I saw a young teenager poking his head around the corner. When I looked at him, he winged what looked like a black rock or piece of asphalt down the road in my direction. As he bolted quickly back around the corner, I quickly realized this was a fucking grenade attack and I made a half-assed attempt to dive down behind these bags of rice on the side of the road.

It went off about 25 feet away and I didn't really feel heat or even think it was that loud. The guys said after the whole thing was over that it was extremely loud. I guess I just had a ton of adrenaline in my system and was so nervous in the moment that I didn't even notice it. I hauled ass to the corner where the kid had thrown it from. I heard my team shouting behind me to keep cover and move into a courtyard instead of crossing into the cemetery. It was a pretty hectic situation and everyone lost track of the possible IED. Instead, we were trying to figure out where and what the explosion was, if there was an ambush or any casualties, or even the exact location of the grenade that went off. Of course, I didn't know any of this was going on. I was just reacting. I moved up with my team as we saw and heard IPs from the rooftop unloading 1000s of rounds into the courtyard VERY close to where we were. They got me on target to see that there were 2 individuals with weapons in the corner trying to cross the street. That's when we took them out. I am thankful because this could have been very different. If it had, maybe I wouldn't have been going home. Word spread pretty fast about my grenade attack. Once I got back, a bunch of people slapped me high five and were saying I was now a member of the "club." I guess they meant the near-death club? Sure, that's cool but with 2 times only a few days,

I think I've had enough! If this place isn't depressing enough, the thought of dying in some freak event doesn't really help. It's not really in my plans. Let's get this shit over with.

SATURDAY 15 JULY

Well, today I feel like absolute shit. I woke up feeling a sharp pain in my lower right stomach. Whenever I move, I start feeling nauseated. I went around 8 a.m. to see if Doc could give me anything. He checked me out and brought me to our head corpsman downstairs. I had symptoms of appendicitis. I ended up throwing up four times in a matter of hours. Our corpsman was in touch with the battalion surgeon over at Fallujah Surgical, who said to give me a few more tests. My blood pressure was extremely low for someone in good health: 50 over 90 (good is 120 over 80).

So, I've made several trips to the porta john and have a trash bag next to my bed. I've just been sleeping and resting when possible. I guess I'm on light duty status for a day or so until this thing clears up or they decide it needs more attention. It's feeling a little bit better now, but I hate getting shit from the guys who say that I'm trying to get out of patrols. This is the first time I've been on "light duty" since boot camp when I got my wisdom teeth pulled. So FUCK THOSE GUYS, especially when it could still be an appendix infection. I'm getting a little rest and I haven't eaten anything because I throw up even when I only drink water. The stomach pain is probably me just being hungry. But this sharp pain sucks and it scares me.

SAT 22 JULY 2006

It's been another week or so. The only new thing was an attack a few days ago. It was 2 RPGs and small arms fire. I was on post and heard rounds crack overhead. It was 5 a.m., so I looked at Kennedy and said "good morning Fallujah." There's a small kitten that came around on one of the posts and we have been taking care of it while we're out there. It makes the 6 hours go by a little faster. Marines will still be Marines, so "USA" has been written on both of its sides and it has a painted eyepatch.

Today, we set in a snap OP, which is an observation post where we hold people in a preselected home hostage so we can be covert and observe high-hostility areas. The goal is to catch insurgents in the act and take them out then or after they try to egress from an attack. I usually try to make friends with the people of the house. I gave some candy and small stuffed animals to the man of the house, who seemed appreciative that I knew some Arabic. He decided that I must be an Elvis Presley and Olivia Newton John fan and gave me two of their old cassettes. I had to take them because it is disrespectful in their culture to decline.

I watched TV for the first time since the Super Bowl in February. I guess Lebanon is getting bombed by Israel? They had better fix their shit because I am not going over there. It looked like a pretty big deal. Anyway, I sat in the sun, baking for hours. We have a heavy patrol schedule coming up, so I'm planning on getting some sleep when I get the chance. This month is almost over, so that's a good feeling. Just a few more to go! It's already August! Like I've said before, rumors say we should be out of here around October 10th or so. A little over 2 months left. Just gotta suck it up. The heat is getting worse, but oh well.

FRIDAY 28 JULY 2006

This week has been pretty intense. There were a few times when we would go on a 3-hour foot patrol to clear a certain part of the city, then get a follow-up mission that would last another few hours. Then, once we got back, we couldn't sleep until our other patrols got back. Here's the kicker: this was all before 10 a.m. so we would start around 3 a.m. What's even better is that we got up the night before to do snap ECPs (entry control points) and BOLO hunts (looking for high value targets or specific people of interest). At times, we were running on 2 hours of sleep, which means we were better off just staying awake, since you feel even more tired with so little sleep.

Also, this week Lance Corporal Landers got shot in the chest, but it was right in the SAPI plate, so the SAPIs did their job. The round hit and deflected off. It did manage to hit his chin and graze him, but he's fine. We had a scare, though, because at first, we were gearing up to go out as a quick reaction team because all we'd heard was that a sniper shot hit someone in the head. In the end, it turned out okay, though.

We are now going into FOB security, which is just standing post doing base security at different areas of our compound, which are made of sandbags and plywood with machine guns. It's boring and makes you tired as hell, but at least it's a break from running around the city. Post can last for 6-10 hours.

I've written a few emails recently, which is nice. The phone sucks and there is only one for the whole company, so it's usually not available. When I'm off and we are not in "river city" (when no satellite phones can be used because someone got injured or killed or a big mission was about to take place or was in progress), the line for the phone can be 6 or 7 people long and around an hour wait. The mail has gotten a lot better, though. Most mail comes within ten days or less, which is better than 2 to 3 weeks.

I'm waiting to find out when we leave this place. I think if we leave here at the end of August, the last month should be a cake walk. I think we'll be at Camp Baharia, with the little huts, palm trees, and nice food. So that would mean 2 or 3 warm meals a day for the last month we're in Iraq! Then I'll be in "I'm going home mode." I heard we'll have only 4-6 days in California and then we will be on our way back to Connecticut!

Things that I'll want first: chiropractor, a dentist visit, massage therapy, getting my hip put back in place, cold bud light, sitting on the family room couch with real dinners, some lovin' from my girl, working on my truck, signing up for unemployment, a vacation, college stuff, taxes, savings. But for now, they're all just part of my daydreams.

SUNDAY 30 JULY 2006

So, we got mortared again today early in the morning. It did little to no damage, which is a good thing. I went on post around 10 p.m. only to see a pretty large firefight in the distance to the north. It went on for about 10 minutes or so with heavy small arms fire. The next day led to two posts of six hours each morning. It wasn't too bad, except for the mortar that dropped about 100m in front of us. Fortunately, it was just a scare.

The main thing about today's post was what I'm guessing were daydreams at 1-2:30 a.m. Maybe it was hallucinations, since I was wide awake. I was also very jumpy, since little sounds or small flickers of light would make me turn around like somebody was walking up on me. My imagination was kicking in and I felt like I was dreaming, even though I was still awake. It was very realistic and clear. I could picture myself with Kacey and it honestly felt like she was right there; the sound and tone of her voice was so real. I pictured an amazing night out on the town and the whole evening all the way through waking up next to each other the next morning. There were some explicit things I don't want my kids read if they ever see this one day. Another dream was really strange. I was in an old-style diner off a small country highway, maybe in Maryland. I was staring at this girl for some reason. I sat by myself in a two-person booth, but when

I finished, I walked up and told her she was the most beautiful person I had ever seen. I told her that I was sorry and that I wasn't trying to hit on her, but that I was from out of town and that something compelled me to tell her that, like she was some kind of angel.

I also pictured my last night with my best friend Kenny. After a night of partying, we'd polished off a 12 pack during the last few hours before I left for the year. We made a toast before each beer we opened. I remember looking over at Kenny in the passenger seat and how nervous I was, thinking about what I was about to go through. Plus, I remembered how sad I was to be leaving my life behind, knowing that my only goal was to make it back to my friends and family. My final dream was about me in a car dealership. I was arguing about how to lower the price on the truck I wanted. I could see myself tearing into the salesman and I might have even scared the guy a little. But the crazy part was that I saw the cars driving by and cars leaving for test drives. Plus, the air was cold and crisp and there were fallen leaves all around, so it was probably in the fall when we'd be back. I know I'm just rambling on, but the dreams were so strange and realistic, I just had to write them down.

The other news that I haven't really mentioned is that we no longer have water. No water for laundry or for showering. The contractors that pump out our porta johns quit out of fear of being blown up, so we had to build our own new place to crap. We have been rationing food out of our storage area to 1 soda, 1 juice, and 1 milk per day (if we even have that much), so we think something is up. We are thinking that either we're going to have to fix this problem or we're going to be leaving this dump and relocating to somewhere else.

TUESDAY 1
AUGUST 2006

I'm sitting here in a house on the eastern-most side of the city. I just finished a two-hour watch, during which I witnessed a firefight near the Blackwater Bridge. Our mission started last night at 2200 hours. Our objective was to maintain a concealed, unknown overwatch position in an Iraqi household that had a good view of the bridge and its tiny outpost that controlled entry to the city. That outpost had been attacked several times in the last four to five days. We've been told that once we get Positive ID (PID) on any aggressors or attackers, most likely fleeing in our direction, we are tasked with a counterattack, most likely in the open field to our east. We're right on the Euphrates River and I found that the night is substantially hotter and much more humid than in the city area where we normally patrol. Also, this house has no source of electricity, so it is pretty rough. We have a watch schedule of two hours on and then four hours off. It's alright, though, because we're it's hard to get any sleep on the cement and mud floors, so we're just as exhausted anyway.

We're supposed to stay covert for three to four days. We only brought enough water for three bottles a day, so rationing is critical. Apparently, we have possibly already been compromised, so we may be extracted and dropped into another location in the area. 13 of us are staying in a two-story building. 5 have to stay upstairs to maintain an overwatch position while the rest stay downstairs. Our command told us to expect fire and contact in the time that we're here. In our location, we have the upper hand, but this is definitely roughing it. 12 hours in and I feel like shit. It's just so sticky, humid and sweaty and on top of that, we have to work around the family that lives in the house. Women can't be looked at and the five kids have to stay in and be contained so they don't go out and tell anybody we're here. It seems similar to house arrest. They can only send 1 adult out with an interpreter that dresses in civilian attire to blend in if they absolutely need food or water This is pretty wild stuff and I know it'll only get worse in the next few days.

WEDNESDAY 2
AUGUST 2006

We got extracted early this morning after I got to know the family pretty well. I'd even been invited to join them for chi and dinner, which is a kind of religious sign of appreciation. Now, we are in an even crappier one-story house where we have a tiny courtyard and sleep on the floor. It's even hotter. I think we will only be here until the morning, so only 3 days total. I think we should patrol back to the CMOC around 3 a.m. This still sucks, though, and it's extremely hot and humid. I want to get back to the CMOC.

FRIDAY 4
AUGUST 2006

This may be my last entry for a while, or possibly ever. There is only so much that you want to remember. Or put in writing, for that matter. It stays in your head and will be there for the rest of your life, so you don't need to save pictures or write it down. It'll always be there. There are things that I'll have nightmares and flashbacks about for the rest of my life. I don't know what it takes for a person to either lose his mind or find peace. I think that I, along with the rest of my brothers here, am completely done, drained, and are running on empty. We are completely spent. Today, we lost a great Marine and a good friend. It was actually yesterday. I really don't want to look back and talk about my fear and my feelings about what happened, but it was one of the worst days of my life. On top of that, my good friend Adam and our Assault Team section leader was also a casualty. Esco got shot in the leg from a sniper, directly shattering his femur. He is lucky to be alive and the last we have heard is that he's in stable condition. Apparently, he'll undergo a pretty intense surgery and will need screws. Esco was in my fire team and was an Assaultman(0351) like me. He was a good friend out here and was always looking out for me. He even helped in a certain situation back home in which I needed someone above me to make something work out. We always joked and he could always make everyone laugh, even in the worst situations. I'm gonna miss the guy, but at least I know he'll be fine.

Sgt. Hoberts was my squad leader from the very first day that I joined Charlie Company after Infantry Training School. He went down in the engagement with some kind of heat-related injury that caused seizures. He was suffering from short-term memory loss and was in a state of shock due to the events. He had a smaller case of this earlier on in the deployment, so we found out he'll probably be sent home to recover. He and Adam are both in the final year of their contracts with the Marine Corps, so they may be done. I want to thank them for everything they taught me and see them again eventually.

Lastly is our friend Burt Fechen. He was killed in action on a patrol in a well-known bad part of Fallujah. It was a sniper attack (one of the many in the last two weeks that have caused a number of casualties and a few close calls). These are the things that you don't see or hear about back home. These are things I wish I never had to see in my life. It's making me sick to think about it right now. I've said my prayers every time I get news like that and realize that maybe I haven't done my part in keeping in touch with God. I don't pray every night, but at the same time I don't want to start just because bad things are happening. However, I don't really know who to turn to anymore. I think I've put myself in a bad spot now, so I am just praying for my safety and the safety of everyone else to get through the deployment and make it home alive. I wish I could do more, but I realize it's all a game of luck. Nothing can or could have stopped any of the horrible things I have seen. Fechen, who I also met and was in my assault squad my entire time in the Marines is now gone and it's hard to think that a good guy like that can be here one second and gone the next.

I shared many good times with him, talking about his old yellow corvette and his back-country Vermont ways. We shared our love of country music the most. During training in the Twenty-Nine Palms, California pre-deployment, we would sit outside, cleaning our weapons and listening to my little wind-up radio that I snuck out to the field. Most of the guys would complain and give us crap about it, but it was something we would bond over. I was looking at some of the pictures and there's one of us sitting on a wall out at Camp Baharia next to the lake. It made me cry, just as it did hearing "Marine Down" come over the net while we were out. We heard 2 WIA and 1 KIA and that was the final thing we heard of our good friend, brother, and Marine Burt Fechen. I really don't know anymore. I sat down in our little chow hall and was trying to eat some food by myself and then one by one, the table I was at filled up with the guys from our platoon. There was some kind of haze around us. It was like we were all completely drained of anything we have.

This is the real Iraq. Make sure when people someday tell you "oh, I was in Iraq," find out what their experiences and what their nightmares were. See if they have had to kill men or see brothers fall. If they say no, then they weren't in the "real" Iraq. I sometimes wonder how it is that only 10 or 20 miles away there are marines riding around on bikes who have TVs, video games, working AC, and even an intramural sports league and hot food every meal while we're here in the shitty city of Fallujah seeing bloodshed every day and none of those perks. We can't even walk outside without our full flak gear and Kevlar on. Mortars can and will hit at any time. We get a shower once every week or so. Not that I really care, but when I wake up each night and smell and hear explosions in the distance, it makes me scared, but more importantly proud of what I am doing.

I know that my job is one of the hardest in the world. I do this so you will NEVER have to see anything like this. From where I'm sitting right now, I don't think I'll want to tell anyone You can read my little journal, but a few guys who I talked that have been here before said, "nobody will ever know or understand what we see or do." That's the hardest part. You get sympathy, but all you want is that they are able to live free and happy lives and don't have to even think about the shit we see over here. You're home in America. Do your jobs, work hard, live free, and be happy. Just know the true meaning to anyone who is in the armed forces, especially the ones on the front lines, who will tell anyone that our mission is to preserve our freedoms so that we can go home and live every day knowing we will never have to be in a place as scary or painful as this. God bless Fechen and his family along with all of our fallen brothers out here. I hate this place, but I will make it home in their honor along with every other marine beside me.

THURSDAY 17 AUGUST 2006

Well, a lot has happened in the last few weeks. I didn't think I would write anything down or even write in my journal anymore, but I guess I still have in the back of my mind that I should have just a small written account of what has been going on. One of the significant events that have happened was foot patrol in an area we knew had a heavy sniper presence that ended up in us taking fire from somewhere only a day after we lost our guys. Foot patrols have gone down, so we have only been doing them in the early mornings. In most cases, we do raids overnight on small houses with intel that they are holding weapons or are places of refuge for the increased insurgent activity. My squad did an operation with the Navy SEALS and we killed 4 insurgent leaders in 2 target houses in that section of the city. We have done 3 other raids that have led us to detaining the #2 and #12 High Value Targets (HVTs) in the Al-Anbar province. We have recovered CDs, computers, and wiring and broadcasting materials that showed anti-American propaganda and footage of insurgent attacks on US and Iraqi forces. We have torn houses apart in our raids. We've been relentless and usually what some people would consider cruel. There is definitely a sense of revenge, hate, and disgust for this country. However, we are doing everything right. We don't go killing innocent people like the headlines seem to make out the Marines do. I think that the loss of our pal Kurt and our other brothers who have been injured and sent to Germany to recover and then go home has fueled our aggression and motivation. We feel pushed to go all out until we leave. Even though this has been a hectic few weeks and we are getting limited sleep and are down a few guys, we still have energy.

Our firm base has been mortared multiple times. One landed only 30 feet from my post yesterday (thank God I was elevated and protected by sandbags). One of our OPs got attacked and a foot patrol from our adjacent unit was attacked and suffered 2 KIA. We took casualties from our 1st platoon: Lauber and Cpl. Barnes, both of whom I was out at the ECP with at the beginning of the deployment. One of our mobile patrols had a grenade attack that was thrown into a turret and exploded, putting shrapnel into the passengers of the Humvee. I was in the area as a gunner when they asked us to attach to their convoy and lead the CASEVAC to the Fallujah Surgical Unit. After talking with Barnes, who was alright, he said that two of the guys were injured really badly and were going to be taken to Germany to fix their injuries and then sent home.

The new threat is that they are moving new extremist groups in and around the city and the violent attacks are picking up. Some of the things I have seen out here, with the disgusting smell of death, decay, trash, and feces, would make anybody sick. At the same time, it makes it scary every time I'm out there on patrol, walking the streets or running from courtyard to courtyard, roof to roof, or barrier to barrier just so I don't end up dead. You become so observant and watchful, assuming that everything you see could blow up or anyone you see could take a shot at you, blow themselves up, or throw a grenade. They all have to have some idea who the bad guys are, but nobody will speak up or warn you. At least in less than a month I'll be seeing the first guys from 1/24, the unit that is replacing us.

MONDAY 4
SEPTEMBER 2006

Everyone in my room is asleep but me. I've had some pretty rough nights' sleep. Three or four hours of sleep felt like ten, but it's broken sleep. I've felt sick, headachy, and weaker because of it. I've felt like crashing and just sleeping for hours, but I can't. I'm writing this because it really is the only thing I can do right now. It's sort of strange today because today there was another memorial service for one of our Marines, Cpl. Jordan Wierson, who was killed in action the day we got back from our 3 days R&R, which pretty much killed the mood. Since then, our company has been in a very different mode. Our platoon has been outside the walls of our compound for 100 hours in the last 4 to 5 days. That comes down to about 5 to 6 patrols per day, sometimes more. Sometimes they are for IED cordons and other times for time-sensitive targets (which is basically an urgent call for a squad or platoon to gear up, run into the briefing room and head to a target house or area to take out a known cell, bomb maker, weapons stash or possible ambush).

It has pretty much broke us all mentally and physically. Not only has there been little to no sleep, poor meals (including only one hot meal a day of slop that comes in those green vats), and countless hours of running around in the burning hot sun in full combat gear, there has been a growing fear of some of the missions we've been tasked with. A few days ago, volunteers were taken for a PSYOPS mission to go on foot. PSYOPS is this dumb thing that the Army came out with recently to imbed into our patrols one of their Humvees that had these huge loudspeakers on it. The loudspeakers would blast out into the city and area we were patrolling, repeating messages such as, "you are pussies if you don't turn in the terrorists in your city, you are all cowards if you try to join the insurgency, we have captured and killed all of these high-ranking Al-Qaeda members so give up," and other jabs at the people. This would piss anyone off, so we're very reluctant to go out there with targets on our chests after the hell we have been through for the past 7 months.

I knew something was up when volunteers were taken. My team of 4 had already said yes, along with a few others. I can't let them be put in danger if I'm not there. The problem was that I went out for a smoke with our intel NCO "Muffin," who told me that there was intel of a planned attack in the next few days. Reports from sources said that it would be a multi-level attack starting with small arms and sniper fire, with a possible catastrophic vehicle-borne IED that would be weighed down with explosives to do max damage. The reason they were asking for volunteers was most likely to clear the heads of all of the officers who knew that something was likely to go down and that casualties were very, very likely. On top of that, this is the same patrol that has gone on the same route, at the same time, on the same day of the week for 5 weeks in a row. Plus, the insurgents were successful in killing a Marine in our adjacent unit that had been on foot.

Despite all of that, it went alright. There weren't any real problems, other than us responding to a firefight where the Iraqi Police had cordoned off a small area where the shooters had run into a mosque that had been completely surrounded. Unfortunately, today, after the memorial service, a convoy heading out to the other FOB (forward operating base) was hit by an IED that killed 3 inside and injured one who was on his way to Germany for emergency surgical life support. This was just hours ago. I don't really know what to say, except that the way they died is horrible and sad. The explosion possibly didn't kill them instantly. Instead, the Hummer went up in flames, trapping them inside as it melted to the ground. It hurts me to think about it and even write this down. Maybe it will paint a picture for somebody, someday, who doesn't really understand what we did over here or asks me "what was Iraq like?" Before you come out with the "did you kill anyone?" question or even the "what was it like?" question, I can only break it down into weird analogies that a normal citizen might be able to comprehend.

I will break it down from the big picture to the small. Imagine yourself in the second-most dangerous place in the world behind Ramadi. This isn't an exaggeration. It's a fact from every recorded attack, including IEDs, small arms, grenades, sniper, beheadings, IP/IA corruption mortars, RPGs, insurgent activity, and the overall hate and discontent of the people, all of which I have seen myself. Now, let's step down. Imagine yourself walking down Main Street with a brother, sister, or someone you love more than life itself and who you would protect at all costs. Imagine a clear, calm day. Then somebody fires 2 shots out of a window or hole in the side of a building somewhere and kills them instantly. Your brother is DEAD. Then, you have to wake up the next day as if nothing happened and walk over that same spot day in and day out. Even worse, there is no time to release your fear or show emotion, because you could be shot as well. You just do it as if nothing ever happened. There is no saying "no" or "I can't" or "I don't feel well." The sickest part is how this draws the person out of our minds and mentally forces you to go about your business day in and day out. That is Iraq.

For you movie people out there, put *Saving Private Ryan*, *Black Hawk Down*, and *Jarhead* together and add 120 degrees, boredom, sadness, the lowest and most helpless feeling in the world, and the most adrenaline-filled thrill ride you can imagine coupled with a crippling loneliness for the entire time you're there. an overall loneliness right alongside you for the entire deployment. Take out Hollywood, add 80 pounds of gear and having to pick your enemy out of a crowd of people that should be grateful for you liberating their city and country. Imagine walking down the street knowing that somebody probably has their sights aimed on your head and is waiting for you to stop moving so they can pull the trigger. Just walking down the street, where every hole or crack in a wall or building that somebody out of view could be waiting for their chance to fire their RPG or take a pop shot at you and your patrol. Imagine sitting in a turret of a hummer going through a marketplace waiting to yell FRAG because a grenade was thrown into your turret and has rolled down inside the cab of the Humvee. At that point, you have 3 to 5 seconds to bail before it kills you and anyone else inside. Even better is sitting on the shitter with all of your gear on, sweating worse than a sauna, just in case a mortar drops on or around you because the enemy has fired from any of the numerous mortar positions in the city, since we are smack dab in the middle of it. Imagine a mortar shell landing near you and sending a basketball-sized piece of shrapnel through the flimsy plastic walls of the porta john. THAT IS IRAQ. I don't know if I'll ever be able to describe it like I just did when asked, but who knows. This is what I'll really want to say.

SATURDAY, 9 SEPTEMBER 2006

Yesterday was another scary day. Our convoy got hit with an IED while sitting in a cordon for another IED on the main road. We started out clearing out a number of buildings that may have had a bunch of explosive materials or a trigger man. It turned into us driving on a side road, going back and forth 3 or 4 times before it blew. After the initial flash came from the first truck, there was a large boom and then a bunch of smoke and dust. The only reason why my team, Team 4-3, wasn't in that truck was because the Captain and his Radio Operator, Whang, wanted to take the lead and we fell in behind them. The blast went off and all I could remember was screaming something about pushing through and seeing if there were any casualties My up-gunner DW said he saw a guy fleeing from a building 75 meters away.

It was so hectic and everything was almost in slow motion because I saw one of my best friends hobble out of the vehicle that was hit and laid down next to a courtyard wall. I tried to get over to him for first aid, but took fire from our own weapons! Rounds from 3 loaded weapons and ammo for the up-gun 240 bravo were all cooking off in the now blazing Hummer. Smoke could be seen from everywhere as the truck continued to burn up. My team got into a courtyard off to the side and once the cook-offs started slowing down (kind of like popcorn slowing down) Johnny Sheehan and I moved up to help see how everyone else was.

On a good note, everyone was conscious. Team leader Jodrey got a small piece of shrapnel in his right knee. Vinny Picard (one of my good friends out here) had a possible broken ankle and pain in both his neck and legs. Driver Pfc. Orel seemed alright but was later treated for a concussion. The Captain and Radio Operator LCpl. Wang were the most seriously hurt with pretty severe concussions. Cpl. Joe turned out to not have shrapnel in his knee. But all of them will be out for at least 10 days. I told them "Team Olbrych is still up, kicking and fighting. They can all sit around but, I'm gonna go continue to fight the insurgency!!" It hurt and was a little difficult to take in afterwards. I may not have a team right now. I'm feeling a little down, but relieved they are fine. It just makes you think what else can go wrong in the last days of our deployment. Just stay strong, hope for the best and hopefully, luck will be on your side…

- The IED was buried under the road
- Found trigger wire that ran 75 M south from blast site into building
- 1 Military age male fled scene
- 1 red Opel Omega seen driving away was engaged by Marines
- Trigger device was a doorbell
- IED was a 155mm artillery shell

Disclaimer: The names of the Marines I served with were altered to protect their identities, since it has been many years since I've communicated with most of them. The Marines who I fought alongside and my brave brothers who gave their lives protecting us will never be forgotten.

Many of us have quietly re-entered society with the hopes of starting new lives and accomplishing new goals. In my experience, it is the combat veteran that struggles the most. This is because the sense of camaraderie and brotherhood will never be the same after the war. Along with this is the realization that the brothers who used to be at your left and right flank are no longer there, as they were in the most ominous times. This ultimately causes the feeling of needing to be on the alert to protect friends, family, and the people around you. Noises, smells, and even just a hunch can bring back the horrors of a firefight or being back on a combat patrol in the middle of hell.

I will forever be grateful for the life I have the honor to live out and will always offer help to any of my fellow veterans. That, often times, is just the ability to be a fellow veteran who is there to listen. This is with the hope that the demons which follow some veterans can be terminated and the vet can once again be victorious in his or her future endeavors.

22 DECEMBER 2018

Hey bud,

So, the Iraq journal just ended. Just like that. I am trying to locate the hard copy version of it to see if there were any missing pages that I didn't get a chance to copy over here. I might have been in the QRF (Quick Reaction Force) at the time I was writing the journal. I would have needed to be ready to move out in a moment's notice. Usually, we would have our gear staged and ready to go so all we needed to do was grab our weapons, ammo and go.

After reading this the feelings I get are still the same. I get a little shaky, a little angry and a little sad. Those months in Fallujah were some of the best and worst times of my life. I had the strongest sense of camaraderie that I think I'll ever have. We were, and still are, brothers. We went through hell together. We were asked to patrol down roads every day where people would be hiding in buildings or setting traps and improvised explosive devices to try to kill us. Think about that for a second. I am now 32. It's been over 12 years and I can still picture most of that city in my mind and would feel pretty confident in getting around if I ever was placed there again.

I had to walk over the same spots where my brothers were killed or injured only days before. I saw the very best and the very worst of mankind. I saw that men are willing to kill one another with no regard for human life. I saw that religion was oddly one of the main links to all the violence in the Iraqi and Middle Eastern fighters. I worked alongside many brave Iraqi Army soldiers who just wanted a better country and a better future for themselves and their families. We weren't so different from us. They had soldiers as young as 16 and as old as 50. They were connected because they wanted a chance at freedom and democracy. The days of Saddam Hussein were over (he was executed only months before we pushed into Fallujah) and the brutal dictatorship was finally over. Now the problem was the never-ending battle for power. That battle would be long and bloody and we still see that region decimated by an unstable government corrupted by terrorist organizations and brutal tribal leaders today.

Today, I tend to have random moments when I'm just thankful to be alive. I think back to my 20th birthday, patrolling Fallujah and realizing I had a good chance of not coming home. Then, patrolling became second nature, the fear left and the aggression and training as a Marine boosted me and the guys around me to do things that most people couldn't even fathom. We walked into battle, firefights, and engagements of all kinds on a day-to-day basis. It became second nature to the point that we were able to be sarcastic about it and almost hypnotized by the need and lust to get out on patrol, to expect contact and meet it with deadly force. We were machines. We were able to push ourselves way out of our comfort zones. The crazy part is that we all knew that we were the only ones there. Trying to describe it or explain the feelings and emotions wouldn't do the experience justice. People back home, friends and family, just wouldn't *get it*. But we're okay with that, because *we* know.

The old cliché of living your life to the fullest and making every day count works very well for me. If I don't focus on being a good person and set goals for myself, I'd probably be like a lot of my fellow Marines who suffer from severe PTSD and depression. Many of the Marines that went through the things I did *and far worse,* find it too difficult to find their place in the normal world. Sadly, I've had to hear of a good number of Marines from my platoon, company, and battalion taking their lives since those early days. The number is extremely high among OIF and OEF veterans, regardless of their branch of service and places they were sent.

I think the only thing I can do to help is to remind fellow vets that this is a great life and we are fortunate to be able to make it special. Instead of feeling sorry for ourselves, we should go out and honor those that made the ultimate sacrifice. Help your brothers and sisters in arms know they are not alone in the fight. Once your service ends, it doesn't mean you can't still provide service to your fellow vets. Be proud and grateful and always to extend a hand to fellow veterans. Have something to live for. Conquer new fears and set out to make small triumphs every day. Hell, this is something everyone, not just veterans can do!

Be a badass, Carson, but be kind, passionate and humble in the process!

25 DECEMBER 2018

Merry Christmas Carson! ....

I am so excited knowing that you're on the way. This is the last Christmas that will be just me and your mom. We still feel like you are a part of this one because you just love saying hi and kicking your mom in the belly! It's so cool and almost surreal when you move around. It lets me know that you're right there, only separated by a small layer of skin. To think we actually have put our hands up next to one another is an indescribable feeling. I'm sure many dads will remember it.

This Christmas we are so grateful for all of the things we have, starting with small things like our health, our family and lots of friends that help and support us! Christmas is about being with the ones you love and sharing the spirit of giving! It's a time to unwind and relax a bit to end the year on a positive note! I spent most of yesterday enjoying my Christmas present from your mom, which consisted of two large storage shelves for our garage. I spent the better part of the afternoon cleaning and reorganizing the garage so everything will be neat and tidy. I also arranged and marked the large plywood window covers that go up during a hurricane. You can never be prepared enough!

This year I want to share a story with you about how special and fortunate I am to be here. When your grandma and grandpa were young, they decided that they wanted kids! They loved each other so much and they were working extremely hard in their careers. It was a perfect time to start a family. This is very similar to me and your mom, actually. Your grandma and grandpa were pregnant with their first child when one day, something wasn't right. Your grandma had to be rushed to the hospital by your grandpa because she was in extreme pain. Your grandpa cared for her so much and knew it was his duty to make sure she would be ok. After some time in the hospital, there was some unfortunate news. Grandma was really lucky, because if Grandpa hadn't taken such quick actions, she could have died. Thanks to him and the brilliance of the doctors, Grandma was ok. However, she found out some bad news. She wouldn't be able to have children due to the complicated procedures that she went through during her stay in the hospital.

The amazing part of this story is that your grandparents, although probably being very upset, didn't give up on the idea of having kids one day! Around the same time, thousands of miles away, across the Atlantic Ocean there was something very similar to a miracle taking place. As your grandparents were staying focused on their goal of having children (even though some people might have given up) a little boy was being taken from the two people who brought him into this world. That boy was placed in a tiny orphanage in Rzeszów, Poland. His birth parents were both unfit to care for a child because of alcoholism, so the state was responsible for taking him into their care. Worse, if you read the paperwork, it clearly states that the parents of the minor child showed no interest in trying to recover their child and maybe turn their lives around. That child was me.

Poland at the time was a Second World country. In the mid-1980s, the country was being heavily influenced by both East and West Germany in a political battle over communism, among other things. The country was still recovering from the devastation of World War II. Poland was just trying to return to a solid and unified nation.

Just when it looked like the story could only get worse, your great-grandparents mentioned to your grandparents that they should adopt, specifically from Poland. Your grandparents went through an intense process of paperwork, fees, meetings, and legal protocol. This led to them being able to take the journey of a lifetime. They flew across the Atlantic to Poland in the hopes of fulfilling their dream of becoming parents. Guess where your grandparents ended up? That's right, in the heart of Rzeszów. After taking a tour of the tiny orphanage and meeting some of the children, it was I, the chubby, blue eyed cutie who captured their hearts. After spending my second birthday with me (I had been in the orphanage for about 1 year at this point) they knew I was the one. Call it fate, call it pure luck, call it whatever you like, but the stars had aligned perfectly for me to be here. Without those pieces falling perfectly into place, you wouldn't be here either. Ask your grandparents for their version of the story if you ever get the chance. Hear it from them directly and you'll understand why I have such admiration for them *and* this life I've been given.

I will leave you with this: you have the chance to do great things. You have the opportunity to live a good, honest, and fair life. You'll have experiences that most people won't. Make them count. I chose to serve this country during a time of war because I love America. I love the freedom that we've been given. I have a chance to do anything I want to if I am willing to work hard for it. I gave up my Polish citizenship around the time I was enlisting in the Marine Corps in order to expedite the process. There isn't a single shred of regret there. As for your grandparents, I love them with everything I have. They have been there for events in my life that will hopefully show them that they made the right choice. I can continue to live a great life because of what they did and more importantly the way they raised me. They taught me so many valuable life lessons that helped mold me into who I am today!

Your grandparents were able to watch me play sports as I was growing up. They drove thousands of miles to make sure I got to whatever game or practice I had scheduled. They devoted time out of their busy schedules to help me with schoolwork and projects and answer my questions about how things work. Your grandparents had to deal with my mistakes and punish me for them accordingly. They got to watch me graduate from high school. Ask them about the funny story about graduation day. It might involve some broken windows, a dead raccoon in the cafeteria, and exposing a certain someone's bare rear end to most of the school! Your grandparents watched as I went off to the toughest basic training in our country at Parris Island, South Carolina where I was molded into a Marine. They also made it a point to be there 4 months later and watch me walk across the parade deck in my service uniform as a new Private in the United States Marines. From there, I would go off to Camp Lejeune, NC and become an Infantry Assultman (MOS 0351).

I went off to war in Iraq multiple times. Each time your grandparents were there to send me off with tears in their eyes, hoping that I would make it back safely. While I was overseas, your grandparents waited nervously for my letters and very rare phone calls. They organized and sent care packages to me and the Marines serving alongside me in Fallujah, Iraq and elsewhere.

After finishing my time in the Marines and receiving my honorable discharge, I attended and graduated from the University of Central Florida. Guess who was right there to watch as former President Bill Clinton read the commencement as I walked across the platform to receive my Bachelors degree in Criminal Justice? Your grandparents.

This story is still being written, however. Just make sure that you talk with your grandparents whenever you can. Learn from them, just like I have. Embrace their willingness to change their lives as well as mine in a matter of moments. Lastly, make sure to say thank you to them and tell them you love them every chance you get. You are now a part of their legacy. You are an Olbrych. I love you, kiddo.

—Dad

30 DECEMBER 2018

Today, I realized we're on the brink of a new year. Crazy, right? In 2019, you'll be here. In 2019, your mom and I will have been married for over a year. I'll change my first diaper and, of course, I'll be turning 33. Three is my lucky and favorite number. So maybe double three will be a good thing. I don't want to get into the whole *New Years* thing yet since I'll probably do that a few days from now! I figured that today I would leave you with some quotes that I have always found the most interesting. Some of these quotes were said by some really influential, brilliant, or just downright strange people. However, since some of the quotes are thousands of years old, they've probably resonated with a lot of people, not just me. So with that, keep an open mind and maybe research the people behind these quotes to learn something. See what was going on in the world when it was said. Look into their lives a bit. Maybe you'll find some similarities. If anything, just know that chances are good that I did the same, considering I have had them written down for years. Without further ado…

"I just want to thank all Marines and veterans past and present for their service to a cause much bigger than their own. We are the 1%."
—unk

"There are only two ways to live your life. One is as though nothing is a miracle. The other is as though everything is a miracle."
—Albert Einstein

"I like to listen. I have learned a great deal from listening carefully. Most people never listen."
—Ernest Hemingway

"Try and fail, but don't fail to try."
—John Quincey Adams

"If something is important enough, even if the odds are against you, you should still do it."
—Elon Musk

"I think the saddest people always try their hardest to make people happy because they know what it's like to feel absolutely worthless and they don't want anyone else to feel like that."
—Robin Williams

"If you hear a voice within you saying, 'You are not a painter,' then by all means paint, boy, and that voice will be silenced."
—Vincent van Gogh

"Never interrupt your enemy when he is making a mistake."
—Napoleon Bonaparte

"A man who dares to waste one hour of time
has not discovered the value of life."
—Charles Darwin

"What I give form to in daylight is only one
percent of what I have seen in darkness."
—M.C. Escher

"One, remember to look up at the stars and not
down at your feet. Two, never give up work. Work
gives you meaning and purpose and life is empty
without it. Three, if you are lucky enough to find love,
remember it is there and don't throw it away."
—Stephen Hawking

"It takes 20 years to build a reputation and five minutes to
ruin it. If you think about that, you'll do things differently."
—Warren Buffett

"What really matters is what you create, does it
work or not? Does it make you proud?"
—Richard Branson

"Give every day the chance to become
the most beautiful of your life."
—Mark Twain

"War is never right but it's a necessary evil. So, hate
the wars but never the ones who fought in them."
—J.Olbrych

1 JANUARY 2019

Happy New Year, little guy! ....

This is where I am probably supposed to write about how impactful this last year was. I'm should write about my New Year's resolutions and make it a point to be better in one or more areas of my mundane life. I suppose I could do that. First, ask me what my last year's resolution was and I'll save you the time while I try and remember. I have no clue! You probably have seen that a recurring theme in my writing has been about self-improvement, chasing dreams, and setting goals.

In theory, I have day-to-day resolution because, I'll be honest, I spend a lot of time making up for dumb decisions, arguments, and choices I make. In most cases, it's with your mom. It's safe to say that I set a new personal goal every week when I do something as simple as break a plate that might have felt like nothing to me. To Susana, that plate was her grandma's that was given to her years ago and had special value that I wouldn't understand. I need to be more mindful of things like that. I have been told by many people over the years that I need to find a softer, more sympathetic side. I agree. I am always fighting to not have the spirit of a crusty old man who's given up on life. In certain situations,I could be much more compassionate, that's for sure. I think your arrival might be the boost I need. I get a little emotional thinking about meeting you for the first time. I relate it to the feeling I get when I remember some of the stories that I have mentioned in this journal.

I am looking forward to being the best father I can be. With that, however, you'll have to give me a chance from time to time! I haven't done this before and I know how I was when I was young. I was a rebel without a cause who was always being pulled back under the gentle custody of my parents. They always seemed to annoy me when I wasn't allowed to do something or when I was in trouble for doing things that were against the rules. Somehow, after a brief period in timeout or a week of being restricted to the house or even my bedroom I would realize, it was probably for the better. During that time, I had time to think about my actions. I had time to work on improving myself by finding crap to do. I'd actually read the books I was assigned. I would do my homework and even the extra credit. Maybe I would listen to different types of music or read some books on subjects that actually interested me like science and technology. There was always a method to my parents' madness and I think it made me a better person. I learned that there were consequences for my actions, just like you will from a very early age!

Back to that whole parenting and fatherly thing I was talking about. I hope you'll go easy on me, at least in the first few years. A baby kind of scares me. You're going to be so damn tiny. I have only held an infant once or twice in my life. Think back to that plate I broke and that should tell you why I may or may not trust myself with holding a football-sized human.

Speaking of football, you will slowly learn that you are coming into a family that loves football. If you want an easier life for yourself, I recommend you side with your dad and be a World Champion Philadelphia Eagles fan! You'll see what all that entails down the road, but let me tell you, you'll be joining some of the best fans in all of sports! And not just in football. Additionally, you've already been given the approval to be a UCF Knights fan by your mother. She caved and got you little UCF booties for when you are born! At the time of this writing, the UCF Knights are playing today in their 3rd ever New Year's Six bowl game. They are riding a two-season undefeated record going into the Fiesta Bowl vs. the LSU Tigers. I don't care who you are, but going on a 24-game winning streak is difficult for even the best teams. That's why it hasn't been done! GO KNIGHTS, your dad's alma mater.

What was I saying about parenting and fatherhood? Yeah, I'm excited. There will be challenges and things I'll learn along the way. It's 2019 and there's this amazing thing called YouTube. I'll be alright. If the cave people did it when they barely had fire, I think I can figure it out! I am more excited to see you progress and develop new skills every day. From crawling, to walking, talking, and potty training. Yay! Then, once the world finds out that you're part genius, part superhero, and world class Olympic athlete, I will finally be able to cash in on the bets I made with friends. *Told you so!*

You're going to be awesome and find yourself. No matter what path you take and which direction you go, I will always be there to support you. Stick to some of the things I've talked about and I'll spend every last breath to ensure you have the ability to chase your dreams and achieve your goals. Be humble, be smart, treat others with respect, don't cheat or steal, earn everything you get. Be generous and help those that reach out to you. Work hard and learn to save. You're going to have the life you decide to make. And remember, you only get one. Love you, kid!

12 JANUARY 2019

What's up Carson,

I'm thrilled to be writing to you today. I'm awake bright and early, thinking about how nice this life is. The New Year is still off to a great start. I just started my second semester towards earning my Master's Degree. I'm in pretty good shape both mentally and physically. Although your mom and I have our moments, I love her more and more the closer we get to our first anniversary. I can feel her rolling her eyes as she always does at any talk of romance and happy relationships that comes out of my mouth. It's true, though. She's still my rock and my happy place even after all the smoke clears and the never ending 180 degree mood swings we both have!

Tomorrow, we are gearing up for the divisional round of the NFL playoffs. Go figure, the Eagles pulled off a stunner at the last second of last week's game against the Chicago Bears. Cody Parkey missed the kick and the Eagles held on to win it. Tomorrow, it's the Eagles versus the Saints, your moms' team! We might have to watch the game in separate rooms! I guess we'll just have to see how it plays out. I have a feeling the Saints might win this one, but don't tell your mom! The Eagles can't keep winning lucky games every week and the Saints are pretty darn good this year!

I'm finally writing a book. Sometimes I go back and reread parts of this thing and can't even believe that I wrote it. That must mean that it is truly from the heart. I have had a ton of support from a few of my close friends who are aware that I am doing this. There were days and months, even, when I wanted to just let it go again for a few more years like my Iraq journal. But I have a new motivation to get this out there for you, myself, and anyone else who might be able to take a small portion for their own inspiration. Sometimes, your own negativity is the only thing stopping you from creating something extraordinary. I think it's fair to say that when a majority of brilliant artists first started out, they looked at others and said "there's no way I could do something like that." Writers, directors, Scientists and famous innovators must all have had moments when they wanted to quit. They must have thought that they couldn't even do what the ones before them had already done, let alone do it better. But they do. They manage to push themselves and accomplish unexpected, revolutionary things, only to realize it was their own minds holding them back.

I'm not comparing my journal to anything great like inventing the wheel or landing rockets on Mars. The moral here is that maybe I should. I should be proud of my work. By publishing this, I know that I will finally have gone the distance and I can say I accomplished what I set out to do years ago. That in itself is enough for me to be at peace.

I love you, my son. Don't compare yourself to others around you but link your heart and mind together and the outcome will speak for itself.

19 JANUARY 2019

Carson,

I want to tell you about a fascinating experience I had that I've never really told a lot of people about. It was a time when I was in the Marines and I was trying to make it home during the holidays. I was stationed at Camp Lejeune in North Carolina and we were given last-minute notice of the actual time we would be released for the Thanksgiving holiday. 4-day weekends were generally referred to as 96's after the number of hours you had off before you had to be back on base.

So, like most of the Marines, I chose to try and book the very first flight out. That flight happened to be around 10 p.m. the Friday evening after we broke from our mandatory weekend liberty "safety brief" formation. Once we were cut loose around 4p.m., I hauled ass to my barracks room where I already had my backpack ready to go. I joined up with a few other Marine buddies of mine who were already planning on getting to the airport in hopes of catching early flights out. Some of them had flights that were scheduled to depart within an hour! As you can see, when the liberty bell is sounded, Marines will try to get every second possible at home to see family and friends!

Once at the Raleigh International, I floated around as, one by one, the Marine guys I carpooled with took off to their respective flights. I stopped by the bar, went out for an occasional cigarette and read a few of the magazines I'd purchased to kill time. I repeated that cycle as 10 p.m. drew closer and closer. Then, I saw the bright read flashing bar run across the tiny blue screen. Cancelled.

My flight was cancelled. Supposedly, there was some bad weather or a technical problem or whatever. I didn't really care to hear the story. All I knew was that I needed to get home and had already purchased a very expensive last minute flight that was now cancelled. I was informed by the ticket counter, that I would be placed on the first flight out at 7 a.m. Just great.

I just continued the laps that I'd already started. The airport wasn't too big, so I decided to just stay in the ticket area, since there was no point in going to an empty terminal or gate. At least there, I could wander outside into the cold North Carolina air and have the occasional smoke. I must have been one of only five people left in the airport, and that's including janitors and a few random security personnel. That's when I met Dan.

It was after 11 p.m. and I had already walked about 10 miles of laps since arriving at the airport. I certainly stood out as a military kid with my high and tight haircut and my over-packed backpack that would just barely pass through as a carry-on! The airport tow truck operator, Dan, who had stopped a few times to get out, stretch his legs, and have a cigarette himself, pulled up next to me once more. We laughed and talk some more about his son, who was also in the Marines, about similar situations that he had experienced. I ended up hopping in the tow truck with the grizzly 60-year-old tow truck operator. We did a few laps, looking for illegally parked cars along the airport's main drag all the way up to the passenger drop off. Dan and I continued to talk about military service, old times, his wife, getting through deployments, and everything in between. Once another hour had passed and it was after midnight, Dan asked what my plan was. I explained that I'd planned on just crashing in the lobby until the gates opened up. After explaining how much I reminded him of his son, the Marine who was stationed in Hawaii, he offered to buy me a meal, since he was getting off shift, and a place to rest for a few hours till he had to be back in at 6 a.m. He said he and his wife wouldn't mind letting me use the little guest room in their home, which was only 10 minutes from the airport.

Dan and I enjoyed an awesome all-American breakfast special at the tiny bar counter of the local IHOP. The waitresses all knew Dan as if he was family. The whole place was empty except for us and a few other patrons. I remember laughing and having a blast. For an old dude, Dan was someone that everyone seemed to love. We finished up and after Dan paid for my meal, we hopped in the tow truck and headed to his home minutes away from the restaurant.

On the way home, Dan explained in a calm but shaky voice that, again, it was his and his wife's pleasure to put up a Marine for a few hours before having to catch a red-eye out in the morning. He made mention yet again of how much I reminded him of his son. We got onto the short stretch of road heading to his house when Dan slowed down from around 55mph to a complete stop. I found this somewhat odd to be honest, I was actually a little nervous. What's wrong? Is the tow truck acting up?

Dan looked over at me and then pointed. We sat there in the shoulder of the road just before an overpass. He pointed, and with a short pause he said, "there, do you see that blue light?" I looked closely while squinting, trying to see some blue light off to the passenger side of the airport tow truck. "Yeah, I see it," I said with a little confusion in my voice. He swallowed and that's when he told me that the blue light was on 24 hours a day and that he stops to say hi every night after his nightly IHOP trip. He explained that the blue light had been put there ever since his son was killed in a car crash only a few years before while on leave from the Marines.

I had cold chills run down my back. We slowly pulled away after a moment of silence and proceeded to his house, where his wife greeted us, asking if I wanted to take a warm shower, have some cookies, a beer, or anything else. After they showed me their mantel, which was full of military awards for both Dan and his son, I was shown to the guest room so I could get a few hours rest before heading back to the airport. Dan and his wife both seemed so happy to help me out, just as they had their own son. A simple, calm feeling of peace came over me as I made it safely and on time to my flight that morning. At the same time, Dan went back to doing his laps in the airport tow truck, just as he always did.

21 JANUARY 2019

One year buddy! We did it! ....

Your mom and I had our one-year anniversary yesterday and it was amazing! It's a simple milestone but, in my mind, it was much more than that. We spent most of Saturday morning outside in this awesome little park near our house on Lake Monroe. For a few weeks, we had been planning on taking some pictures of the pregnancy and wanted to wait for the perfect day to do it. On top of that, your mom ordered some beautiful dresses online so she could really shine for our photo shoot. The key part of this whole outing was that yours truly was the photographer. That's right, since we'd bought dresses for the photoshoot, we decided to save some money and take the photos ourselves. To accomplish this, we had to purchase a tripod that would accommodate a smartphone, since that's how we would be taking the photos.

As the newly appointed professional photographer, I felt the need to go all out. This meant ensuring we both had a few different outfits, some water bottles, and even some hand towels in case it got too hot and we needed to wipe sweat away. I took this new promotion to another level and made sure that I packed a small bench and blanket that we could use as props. Mind you, the only real photography experience I have is snapping a crap load of photos while on vacations or being obnoxious with my phone camera while out partying with friends. I'm an amateur to say the very least. The only real experience I had were the amazing engagement and wedding photos that we'd had professionally done!

I'll tell you what, your mom looked absolutely stunning. She'd recently had her hair colored, so it was fresh and very dark brown. She started off wearing a long, flowing red dress that made her shine in the mild Florida winter weather. I had scoped out the location for the shoot and I think it only enhanced her beauty. She wore a striking, all-natural looking crown of white flowers to go with her red dress. I tried my very hardest to stick to my natural, goofy, clumsy self so that she would be happy and go along with my ridiculous attempts to look like the movie portrayal of a photographer. Behind the laughs and occasional tripping over myself, I found myself just watching her look so peaceful and natural, which reminded me how lucky I was to have such a beautiful wife. You might think I'm just saying that to get brownie points. But guess what? I don't care. Maybe if you're lucky, you'll be able to look at the pictures yourself someday! Your mom is a saint!

The best part of the whole thing was the fact that we just had so much fun. We had a tiny clicker so that we could both be in the pictures together. I would have to set the camera up just right with your mom waiting in a pose for me to run over and puzzle piece my way into her statuesque position. It was a blast. I don't know if she'll tell you otherwise, but this is my story and I say I was a damn good photographer!

After finding a few other locations to take some more fun pictures, we called it a day. We drove the easy five minutes home after stopping to grab some Publix subs and sushi for your mom. Hopefully, you'll enjoy sushi so she can have someone to indulge with her! I knew she must have been happy, because she couldn't put down her phone after we packed up the photo equipment and all my makeshift props. Once we got home, she immediately pulled up the pictures on our big screen TV to review them and pick out her favorites! She might not have said anything officially, since she never likes to let me win, but I know I did well! It's the little things, Carson. Days like that will stay implanted in my heart and soul for the rest of my life. And guess what? You were there too!

Love you big guy. Less than 2 months now!

29 JANUARY 2019

Dear Carson,

Today is a good day. I didn't do anything all that exciting. or accomplish anything more than usual. I have adopted a saying that I will officially give credit to my good friend from work, Tim Bull. I get more things done by accident then most people do on purpose. I try to fulfill that saying by thinking that there is always something you could be doing, plain and simple. If it's not at work, it's at home, or on the way home. Expand your mind, get creative, read something, call an old friend or family member you haven't talked to in a while. Plan a trip, search the internet for random crap or answers to questions you have. Speaking of which, try to remember things throughout your day that might have discovered you that didn't know much about. Write them down and look them up later. Do some chores, get some exercise, offer to help someone, even if it's something they can do for themselves.

Today is a good day. This weekend, we had your baby shower and it was so special. It started with your grandparents flying in on Wednesday night last week. It's always so exciting to see them, since I miss them more than I suppose I let on. They flew down from Connecticut to escape the sub-ten degree weather. Yeah, tell me about it! Why do you think your dad made the decision to move down to Florida as soon as possible? I only wish I could see my family more. That includes my aunt, uncle, and all my cousins. I feel like I tend to miss out on important events and as much as I talk about always taking care of your family, I do sometimes wish I could be closer: only a call away if I was needed. Maybe it's a Marine thing, maybe it's just good morals, I don't know.

One of the other awesome parts of the long weekend was the fact that I was able to take your mom and grandparents to St. Augustine for a beautiful 75 degree sunny day. The oldest town in the United States, only about an hour away from us, never fails to impress. It was really special to spend quality time with my parents and see them so happy. On another day, we made a trip out to Mt. Dora. It's a quiet little town in the middle of nowhere with lots of tiny little shops located right on a beautiful lake. Just being able to take in this special time with my parents is priceless. I'm trying to let them know that they've done an amazing job making me into the man I am now.

I see it in my mom's eyes sometimes. Sometimes, she says just the right thing to remind me of when I was little and then throw in a little piece of encouragement about the job I'm doing now as an adult. Pops, your grandpa, is someone I always wanted to make proud by trying to show him how knowledgeable of the world around me I am. I tend to find myself trying to show off as a way to get his acceptance of little things. I can tell that when I do that, he knows in his mind he's taught me quite a bit. I do a lot of things now exactly like he did them when I was a kid.

The baby shower was hosted by our good friends, Jeff and Melyssa, along with your aunt Kristen. They were awesome and made the day just perfect. The whole thing was dinosaur-themed because I like dinosaurs more than a normal adult should! I hope that we'll have that in common, or else I'll have a lot of your gifts to play with myself! We had around fifty people packed into our house to enjoy a fun day relaxing and to celebrate the fact that your almost here. All of our friends and family were so generous. They got us gifts of all kinds. I'd say that for at least half of the things we received for you, I'll have to do some serious research to learn how to use it. I also got a lot of advice from our friends on how to be a good father. I couldn't be more grateful for everyone's support. By the way, your mom looked stunning. That was also one of the best things about the party! She always finds a way to keep me smiling!

Today was a good day. I was having some doubts and have been contemplating changing majors for my master's degree. I'm getting straight As for the first time in my life. Seriously, I was a B, C, and a random-A-in-some-odd-ball-class kind of a student all my life. So why have I been fighting with myself over Contract Management or Project Management degrees? I guess I'm just afraid of failure or of not understanding everything I'm learning. I'm able to artic-ulate it well enough to write the average 15-page term paper and case study. I passed all my midterms and finals with As. I just have felt dumb because the people in my classes all seem to have pretty diverse backgrounds in contracting. Beyond that, it's kind of boring! So there you go, I gave you all the reasons why I wanted to just give up and switch to something else that I *think* will be more fun, *maybe* easier, and what-ever else I made up in my head. I made some phone calls and wrote emails to a handful of people at Florida Tech so I could meet with an advisor to complete the process.

Then, it happened. The hints were all there. The "prac-tice what you preach" voice in my head screamed at me while I was on my way to work. So much so that I got pulled over for speeding and got a nice $166 ticket for going 15 miles over the speed limit! What does that have to do with my master's degree dilemma? Because shortly after the embar-rassing, lesson-teaching moment, I heard something on the radio. The radio host quoted something, out of the blue, but so incredibly relevant to my life, that it resonated with me all day. "85% of what we worry about never happens."

We spend a lot of time worrying about stuff that is almost pointless. I realize that everyone I come into contact with has some kind of worry in their life. For me, there are tons of worries: family, health, money, work, career, *school*! Really, my fear about not understanding or being as smart as my classmates was enough to make me go through hoops to research different master's programs? It's funny, it didn't hit me until after lunch that I was still worrying about my school stuff. I had submitted a term paper two nights ago and felt *ok* about it, but not much more than that. But I kept thinking about that quote, enough that I knew I needed to write about it tonight when I wrote to you.

Another fear ran over me. Am I ever going to finish this book? Will I finish it before you're born? Oh God, how will I end it? Yeah, welcome to my life! I got advice from my parents while they were visiting. I got advice from Tim at work. Even your mom said, "what are you worrying about with this damn class thing for, just do it" days ago. Then, while in the shower only moments ago, I was on my phone looking up my classes. Yes, maybe you didn't hear the part about me always trying to do *something*. Well, when something is on my mind I try and do two or three things at the same time to be more productive. I guess this time, it worked. While taking a steaming hot shower and wiping the fog that settled on my phone screen, I saw it. The grades were in for the case study I'd had my doubts about. 100%. Perfect score. That decided it: stay the course. Be great in the things you are afraid of and try that much harder to prove to yourself that you *can* be great. The things you fear might just push you to take them head on instead of run from them. And that's exactly what I'm going to do, buddy!

I love you, Carson!

4 MARCH 2019

Hey Carson,

Dad's been busy. Pretty obvious, since you can see the date. A lot has been going on in my life, your mom's life and, well, *your* life! Dude, you're less than two weeks from getting your first glimpse of the world. I realize that my mind, body, and soul have literally taken over and I am just a morph of a human right now. I think knowing that you are so close to being here in my arms has made me go a little crazy. I can't quite explain it, but it's like I can't stop moving, thinking, working, talking, and all the other *-ings* that are out there. I think my mind is not letting me hone in on the fact that I am about to be a dad.

I decided to rip up the kitchen about a week ago, so now your mom hates me. Who in their right mind tears out a kitchen all the way down to the cement floors only weeks before their first baby is due? Meanwhile, I had two midterms and homework assignments in my Master's courses. I've also had to hold down a job where there are only about three of us doing what six people normally do. Oh, did I mention your mom? Yeah, by the grace of God, I've somehow kept her sort of happy. Scratch that, I'm pretty sure she had a meltdown when she walked in to find the entire kitchen missing. However, I do give her credit, she kept it inside her head. That's the sort of thing she would usually rip my head off for. Unfortunately, that means that she must be really tired and doesn't have the strength to battle me and my spontaneity. I tend to always find some kind of project and not quite finish it. She keeps saying that the stress I cause is going to make you come early.

It seems like over the last month, you have been wanting to escape anytime that I am spending a relaxing time with your mom. She's so darn cute and she usually thinks I'm kidding when I tell her. I think she feels fat or something. In reality, your old man has actually put on a little baby bump of his own. That kind of sucks. The last few weeks, I've been all about running around trying to get things ready for you. Your mom has been working really hard to put the finishing touches on your room. She spends at least half her day on Pinterest and Amazon. I, on the other hand, am doing manual labor, slaving away to bring home a paycheck and support this family! That's maybe a bit of an exaggeration. But just know, your pops works pretty darn hard.

I had all this awesome stuff in my head when I was driving to work that I wanted to talk to you about. I suck. I can't remember much of it, so I'd rather not force it. I know I find myself at my desk at work from time to time, upset that I don't write to you as much as I want. In fact, I ruined my "one letter a day" idea about 5 days into this wild, twisting and turning jumble of words on paper. The only thing I can think of is to stay true to the person I am. I thought about cheating. That's right, I was going to write a bunch of letters and try to back date them so that it would look like I was more put-together. I wanted to show you that your dad can actually commit to doing something 100%. Then I realized that it's not cheating, it's actually just the way the cookie crumbles. Really. I honestly spent the last month and a half trying my best and giving 100% in most of the things I was working on. Yes, I said most. I can always work on being a better husband (I only have a year and change of practice) and a better listener. But for now, I am truly just living. It might be a little sooner than I'd like, but I am dreaming of that moment when I can just slow down, smile and look at you and realize the next chapter is just beginning. I promise to love you and your mom with everything I have. There will be ups and downs. We will be a team. We'll teach each other things. We will always work hard and make sure we understand true family values. My goal is to help give you the tools you'll need to be an intelligent, honest, and hard-working young man. Work hard so that one day you won't have to call it work and you'll simply call it living.

I love you, Carson. I have a feeling this theatrical roller coaster of a book is drawing to an end. It would just help if your dad could remember everything he envisions in his borderline crazy mind. Only 16 days!

9 MARCH 2019

Hey Bud,

That's another week down. I finally wrote some things down that I wanted to make sure I write to you before this book is finished. It starts with what I look at every day when I walk into work and sit down at my desk. I have typed up in small font and printed out little quotes and notes that help me slow down and take in the moment. Taped under my computer monitor is:

Ask better questions, write more, do something generous, help someone who wasn't expecting it, do something spontaneous, learn something new, take 15 minutes to enjoy some peace and quiet, explore.

This is all written on a little note card so I can see it from time to time throughout my day. Both quotes from my journal are typed up, printed out, and taped to the wall to my left in small, size 12 font:

"Is it that while your life was easy, I walked along your side; But here, where the walking was hard and the path was difficult, the times you needed me most, those, my son, those are the times in which I carried you"-Footprints

*"I loved every firefight I was in because for those brief
seconds nothing else matters. It all comes down to
the fact that you are going to die if you don't kill this
guy and that's it...And all I have to do is live."*

Finally, in another spot that is taped right under my phone:

"Don't worry about it, it'll be alright..."

It might not seem like much, but those little notes to
yourself might make more of an impact than you think.
Ultimately, it's up to you to direct how your day is going to go!

If you need help, ask for it. You would be astonished at
how many people feel humbled when they have the opportunity to help.

If you want something or have your mind set on a certain goal, you have to make yourself noticed. People aren't
going to come and seek you out; you will have to pursue
them to ask for their guidance and how to get those things
which you desire.

Don't assume that anyone knows what your goals or
intentions are.

Understand death. Every man dies, but not every man
really lives. *Make sure you look that line up and watch the asso-
ciated movie. It is one of the all-time greatest!*

You are going to change your mind a lot. That's okay.
Go with what your gut tells you.

Run with new ideas, dreams, or visions. You never
know where they'll lead you. You'd rather risk failing than
not trying at all and living with regrets.

Growing older, I have flashbacks. I have crazy dreams
where I feel like I'm back in middle school sometimes.
Sometimes, I'm standing watch on a machine gun tower.
Other times, I'm just a little boy at a trade show with my dad.

Sometimes, I'm in the backyard. I'm just running around, playing hide and seek with my little sister. These flashbacks are the best memories that I didn't even know I had.

I also see myself doing some of the dumber things I've done. Like the time I got naked and did jumping jacks in the rain to show off to a bunch of seniors on our senior skip weekend. I recall getting up on the cement wall and taking a selfie looking down the center part of the Hoover Dam. Granted, I drove out there with my friend after a wild night in Vegas just because we felt like it. We pulled over around 3 a.m. and I took a leak right off the side. It's a long way down! In my inebriated state, I also realize now that I am pretty lucky that I'm still here to talk about it! Ferris Bueller said, "Life moves pretty fast. If you don't stop and look around once in a while, you could miss it." That couldn't be more spot-on.

Get a dog. You'll never understand love until you get your first dog. Understanding what a dog's love is to you might help you someday understand what real love is when you need to make some big choices. A dog's purpose is to love you, be there for you, comfort you, and earn your trust. Having a dog gives you a purpose and is a huge step in understanding responsibility for something other than yourself. In fact, I recommend a book called *The Art of Racing in the Rain*. This book might seem like it's for you and in some odd way I feel like it really hit home for me.

Understand money. Make sure to understand that personal finance is part of your personal responsibility. Read the book *The Total Money Makeover*. That book and the lessons within it will help you be successful and understand budgeting. The end goal is achieving financial peace. With any luck, they will teach you about finances in school, since that will help you in life a great deal. You don't always have to have the biggest, newest, and best thing on the market. When you work hard for something, save your hard-earned money, and then go purchase it yourself, it will feel a lot better than for a person who has it given to them, or worse, go into debt for it.

Hopefully, the school system and the style of teaching might change. Hopefully, the curriculum will swing in a direction that will allow you to start pinpointing your ideal professions at an earlier age and you can learn about them rather than learning about things you don't need, such as underwater basket weaving and 19th century literature in Germany. It would be a lot more applicable to actually learn about careers and professions before you're making decisions about what you want to study in higher education, like college or a Master's or Doctoral degree.

Maybe one day, I won't be able to remember the good times, the bad times, or any of this. It's possible the stories and the memories I have may get lost in the years to come. Maybe one day, you'll be by my side, just like I plan on being by yours. You'll read every word of this book and make sure I remember and understand the lessons that I tried to convey. Maybe I'll find peace knowing that you have learned a few things from your old man. Maybe then I'll have really lived. Maybe then I will have found my purpose. I originally planned on writing this book for you, but maybe in reality, I'm actually writing this for me!

I love you, Carson.

20 MARCH 2019

Hey little man,

Today is officially 40 weeks! Susana is full term. So, what does that mean? I guess it means that you're going to be here soon. The crazy part is that we thought you might be here already. Your mom went to a doctor's appointment on Monday to see if you were ready to go. Without getting too graphic, we'll just say that you needed a few more days! Man, your mom is a champ! You keep kicking her and moving around so much. She says it goes on all day long while she's at work. You know what I just realized? You're going to be an Aries, just like your dad. Oh boy...

That means a whole lot of things! You are going to have the warrior spirit and be full of adventure. You won't settle on anything easily. You'll love a good argument and will want to win at all costs. You will be pretty headstrong and love to challenge yourself and others if given the opportunity. You may find yourself always needing to hide your fear.

It might be possible that you'll get yourself into some tough situations because you think you're making the right choices but will be too stubborn to admit that you're wrong. You'll need an assortment of friends and co-workers around you because of your wild spirit and ever-changing moods. You might change direction physically and mentally numerous times throughout the day or in a simple conversation. You'll find yourself always fighting for people that you care about. You'll do everything in your power to not hurt anyone you cross paths with. However, that temper, that alpha mentality, may show its ugly face and you'll get the fight or flight instinct time and time again. That may be a flaw or it might be one of your greatest assets. You'll just have to learn how to harness that.

Son, you might be wrong. You might make a bad choice. However, once you realize it, own it, figure out a solution, and make sure you confront it head on. If you try and hide it or lie about it, the backlash might be much more than you can handle. I am not talking about physical pain. However, it could come back to haunt you in forms of regret and embarrassment. That would be the worst part.

You'll be very instinctual and full of imagination. You'll have a free spirit and want to take on the world. I know that I always found myself questioning everything and staying quiet until I had a grasp on the situation. You won't want to look dumb, so you'll be a very good observer. One of your best skill sets will be the ability to sense a good or bad situation. However, you might have the "get up and go, do it now" attitude which may make you overlook some small details. It'll be ok because your intuition and ability to adapt will take you very far.

Be fearless, but don't let everyone see it. Have a subtle confidence that will make people believe in you. Be honest and trustworthy so that those around you will be willing to confide in you. You'll get some of the greatest pleasures in life just by knowing that you can be someone people trust with often very sensitive things.

A final thought is to try and keep your promises. You'll engage your brain all the time. You will know you can help in many situations. Instinctually, without as much as a blink you might want to dive right in to assist. You'll have a solution and know the answer often.

However, a huge downfall will be the feeling of not being able to keep your word or promises. I have that weakness and it's something you should try to work on as soon as you understand it. If you try to take on too much, too fast, too often, you'll break promises. You might miss due dates or fall behind. At times, you may take on something new without remembering the other things you'd already started or promised to be a part of. In the process, you may hurt people or even worse hurt yourself trying to make up for it. The worst feeling is guilt and realizing you let people down. So, work hard to make promises that you know you can keep. That Carson, can make you physically and mentally a strong young man!

Hey, Champ! ....

You should probably come out soon! I am running out of anxious dad chores to do. More importantly, your mom is having to lug you around as you get bigger and bigger! I know you're only a few days past your due date, but help me out here, buddy! I feel you kicking and squirming around. That has to mean that you are wanting OUT! Susana is doing a pretty good job of being tough, but I know she is more than ready. Surprisingly, she has been trying very hard to have a positive and not angry attitude, which I can't say I would be able to do if I were in the same position. She still looks adorable and gives me that cute little smile a few times a day, which makes me want to keep working hard to make everything perfect for our little family.

Since you have decided to extend your stay, I've tried to keep busy at home. I've pressure washed the entire driveway. I have organized the garage at least three times. I've gutted and had the entire kitchen remodeled with all new cabinets. I have purchased all new pool equipment and worked on making the pool flawless and crystal clear. I have to say, your mom lucked out with having such a hunky pool boy! I've continued on with my Master's degree. I am kicking ass at work, which feels pretty good. Often, I struggle with not having my work go recognized. However, I just push on anyway. I've learned to just work hard and at times, accept simple compliments from students in my classes letting me know that they enjoyed or learned a lot from the class. I have gone to lunch with my co-worker Tim, who has always tried to help keep my spirits up and to remind me that there are plenty of things that are out of our control and that we can only control how we work and interact with people. He finds peace in painting all types of amazing things in his off time. In fact, he is working on something special just for you! In my off time, I am working on projects around the house and just enjoying some quiet time with your mom sitting around the pool. Oh yeah, and I decided to write this book!

I think you are going to be here within hours from now, so I think I need to go for a quick motorcycle ride or for a walk with the dogs. It's so exciting and all I can think about is how my life is going to shift direction yet again. I can't wait to give you a chance to experience the world. I will make it my duty to teach you as much as I possibly can so that you can learn to make your own decisions. I want you to learn lessons and find passion in trying new things. You shouldn't live under a rock, as they say! Get out and explore! I want to try very hard to have fun family adventures from time to time. I also believe that if you work hard and go above and beyond that there should be recognition. It shouldn't be expected, however. I will make it a point to let you know that I appreciate it or adversely, when you have *done messed up boy!*

I love you kiddo, see you *very* soon!

25 MARCH 2019

CERTIFICATE ....

The State Orphanage in Rzeszow, ul Nizinna 30, certifies that a minor child Marcin Michal Musiuk comes from a pathological family (alcoholism). The boy has been staying in our orphanage since the 16th day of September, 1986 and since that time nobody from his family took any interest in his being. His parents did not maintain contract with him.

In connection with that, the State Orphanage in Rzeszow made a petition for depriving his parents of their parental rights. Mr. Ireneusz Masiuk and Mrs Maria Masiuk have been deprived of their parental rights over their minor child Marchin Michal Musiuk by virtue of a Decision of the District Court in Krasnystaw, Files No III R Nsm 32/87 of the 27-th day of November 1987

Rectangular seal with the following inscription: "Director of State Orphanage, Zofia Czekaj" and Undecipherable Signature"

Decision

On the 12-th day of April 1988, District Court in Rzeszow,
Court Division for Family and Juvenile Affairs,
In the branch composed of;

Presiding Judge: Wieslawa Kosik, Judge of District Court
After examining, on the 12-th day of April 1988
in Rzeszow, a case coming on to be heard upon the
petition of Kenneth Olbrych and Betty Olbrych ,
for adoption of a minor child Marcin Masiuk,

Decides:

To decree the adoption of minor child Marchin Michal
Masiuk born on the 5-th day of April 1986 in Krasnystaw, the
Certificate of Birth no 476/1986 being issued by the register
of vital statistics in Krasnystaw, by Married Couple Kenneth
Olbrych and Betty Olbrych, Marietta, Georgia, USA.
To change the first and middle name of the adopted minor
child from "Marchin Michal" to "Jonathan Wilson"
This decision certifies the official adoption of minor
child Jonathan Wilson Olbrych. This adoption
causes the full legal consequences according to article
121 of the Family and Guardianship Code for Full
Adoption given this 12th day of April 1988.

At first glance, this might sound like a sad story. But in reality, this is where my story starts. It starts out as a very long shot that a tiny baby who was taken from an alcoholic family half a world away in a tiny village in Poland, can still have a chance. That chance started with two loving parents taking a chance and following their hearts. That chance started in the United States of America. The land of opportunity, the land of one and a million chances. But I don't take one day for granted and know that, through my life experiences and fighting the war in Iraq, every day is special.

My mom and dad need to know that I am grateful for the life I have been given. There are no words that will ever be able to let them know my sincere appreciation for the lessons they have taught me over my lifetime. The only true way to thank them is by continuing to be a great person, a devoted husband - and now a father. I will pass on many of the valuable life skills I learned to Carson, as well as implement some of my own. The spirit of my parents will carry on because the true legacy every person has is knowing that they made an impact. In this case, I was able to hopefully have an impact on a lot of people over the years. Therefore, in a roundabout way, my parents can rest easy at night. Their legacy will be the one I pass on to Carson!

So, maybe one day, Carson, you will be able to pass this story onto your son or daughter. Maybe you'll be able to make a difference in the life you have. Hopefully, you'll learn a little along the way from your old man! I just hope I can do as good a job as my parents did for me.

Well, now it's time to go to the hospital. Your momma has an appointment and we won't be leaving till we have you in our arms!

I love you, Champ!